Speak for a Living

The Insider's Guide to Building a Speaking Career

Anne Bruce

ASTD
PRESS

Alexandria, Virginia

ASTD Press is an internationally renowned source of insightful and practical information on workplace learning and performance topics, including training basics, evaluation and return-on-investment, instructional systems development, e-learning, leadership, and career development.

Ordering information: Books published by ASTD Press can be purchased by visiting our website at store.astd.org or by calling 800.628.2783 or 703.683.8100.

Library of Congress Control Number: 2007931360

ISBN-10: 1-56286-508-0
ISBN-13: 978-1-56286-508-5

ASTD Press Editorial Staff:

Director: Cat Russo
Manager, Acquisitions and Author Relations: Mark Morrow
Editorial Manager: Jacqueline Edlund-Braun
Editorial Assistant: Maureen Soyars
Retail Trade Manager: Yelba Quinn

Copyeditor: Phyllis Jask
Indexer: April Davis
Proofreader: Ann Bruen
Interior Design and Production: PerfecType, Nashville, TN
Cover Design: Rosemarie McLeod
Cover Illustration: iStockphotos.com

Printed by Victor Graphics, Inc., Baltimore, Maryland, www.victorgraphics.com

CONTENTS

FOREWORD

From the perspective of a speaker bureau owner for more than 15 years, this is a *must* read if you want to become a successful professional speaker and trainer. This book is the blueprint for your speaking career. There are not many books on this subject because no one has devoted the time or effort to such a task. Yet, everyone thinks he or she can speak because professional speakers make it appear easy. Just think, someone will pay you for talking! The reality is that this is hard and grueling work. As Anne has so vividly stated, "If you don't have the stomach for this crazy ride, then you may not be cut out for the speaking and training profession."

There have been many speakers and trainers who have gone by the wayside because they had neither the staying power nor earned the money with abundance. This is a business and it has to be treated as one. You will spend hours researching, compiling, reading, studying, and rewriting your stories until you want to scream. Yet, you will continue to polish your speech because it is your *only* marketing tool. If you do not receive immediate rewards such as spin-offs, then something is amiss—and then you're back to the drawing board again and again until you get it right.

Once you have honed your speech, you need to market yourself. Anne has outlined this avenue beautifully for you. You can be the best speaker in the world, but if you cannot market yourself—sell yourself and make cold calls—then you are in trouble. You may want to consider a marketing manager to assist you in your marketing efforts because this is the tough part of any business. What makes *you* so different from all the other professional speakers and trainers on the circuit today? Anne helps you find your "true north" in this guide to professional speaking and training.

Anne Bruce has encapsulated in this book what it takes to be successful in speaking and training. Read and learn from her varied experiences and mistakes; she has ridden the roller coaster and survived! Use this book as a daily tool to launch your career in speaking and training. Anne will make your life easier as you begin your new career. Heed every chapter; savor it because it can make a difference in your success as a professional speaker and trainer.

Betty Garrett
President and CEO, Garrett Speakers International, Inc.
former president, Meeting Professionals International,
Dallas/Ft. Worth Chapter
May 2008

PREFACE

You can make a million dollars as a professional speaker and trainer.

If you want to ask me, "Anne, do you make a million dollars or more a year as a professional speaker and trainer?" go right ahead. The answer is *no*.

I do, however, make a darn good living. I pay my bills and I live in a lovely home with my husband, David, in the charming community of Charleston, South Carolina. I take annual mother-daughter trips with my daughter Autumn from Honolulu to Paris. I drive a nice car and I am blessed with more possessions than one person needs in a lifetime. I make my living as a professional speaker and trainer, and I love it!

I wrote this book because I saw the need for a practical, real-world tool that can help people like you to build a thriving speaking and training practice. Just as doctors or lawyers build their practices over time, so do professional speakers and trainers. And just like any other profession that helps others, the reason you go into a business like this one is to (in the words of famous speaker Zig Ziglar) help other people get everything they want in life and more. Real pros know that when they have this intent, the minute they step out on a stage or into a classroom, they also will get everything they desire as a speaker/trainer and more. That's the magic of this business. It's a business where success is built on the authenticity and genuine intent of the presenter. That's you.

If your ultimate goal as a professional speaker and trainer is to become rich and make a million dollars a year traveling the world, that is a fine and respectable goal. I know many people in this industry who do just that. But here's the catch. All of them seek first and foremost to serve their audiences and enrich others with the information they've formulated to share within the context of a platform speech, training session, or one of the many other formats available to them—all of which I will go over with you in this book. My point is that your initial intent and desire to help others to help themselves is what counts. From that point you can decide that you want to make 10 million dollars a year in this business. That's up to you. But the original focus has to be enhancing the lives of your audience and the people you are training and to whom you are speaking. Your effort must be audience centered, not speaker centered, if you want to succeed.

I am confident that if you start out in this business with this goal in mind, you can achieve more success than you ever imagined possible in the lucrative world of speaking and training. From this platform of success you can expand your world to include authoring books, creating product lines, being a life coach or consultant, teaching internationally, and building the professional speaking career of your dreams.

The Approach and Purpose of This Book . . . .

I wrote this book because, as someone who makes her living as a professional speaker and trainer, I am constantly being asked by people how they, too, can get into this business and make a living speaking. Let me say this: It's one thing to do a speech for which you are compensated one or two times and quite another to ride the roller coaster ups and downs of this crazy industry and survive and thrive in it for 10 or 20 years.

There are lots of *you-can-do-anything-you-want-in-this-life-even-though-you're-not-qualified-to-do-them* books out there. These books often preach the same sermon to everyone from the household plumber to the kindergarten teacher. The message is that they can quit what they are currently doing to support themselves and launch into the professional public speaking and training profession—and that all of this can be accomplished with little or no experience—and then that person can start raking in millions of dollars a year. I disagree. I do not believe that just anyone can do this kind of work. Even if you are a published author, that's no guarantee either. In fact, most authors I know are not necessarily riveting speakers.

That's why you'll find in this book an important questionnaire that will help you to reveal if, indeed, you are truly cut out for this profession. You may or may not like the questions, but answer them all and be honest with yourself. For example, a lot of people fail to realize how physically grueling this life can be. Many of us are on the road a good deal of the time, flying 80,000-plus miles a year, lifting and carrying boxes and training materials from our hotel rooms to our training rooms and back, running to and from airport gates, standing on our feet for 12 to 14 hours a day at conferences and book signings, and setting up and cleaning up training rooms long after the class has adjourned. Yes, the trainers clean the classrooms. Does this mean you have to be able bodied to do the job? No! I work with disabled presenters who have more energy than I'll ever have. But they accept the grueling part of the work and make accommodations for it and keep moving, never whining or complaining. This is not a business for martyrs. In many other professions, people often complain endlessly about how tired their jobs make them, but when you're in this business, you are always *on*. Everyone looks to you to set the example and to be the beacon of light that draws people in. There's no room in the professional speaking arena for complainers or prima donnas. We all learn to go with the flow in this business (and it is a business first and foremost), and when things don't go as planned, our audiences don't have a clue. Why? Because the real pros make it all appear seamless by virtue of their fortitude and attitude. I'll address this later in the book, as well.

My 15 years of experience in this business have enabled me to create this real-world guidebook for actually starting your own speaking and training practice by using my four-step approach to success. I guarantee that after reading this book, you will have a good idea if this profession is right for you—and if you are right for it.

Not only will you get the strategies and lessons I have field-tested time and time again in hundreds of seminars, workshops, and international conferences, but you also will gain a powerful course of action that will allow you to navigate the sometimes turbulent waters of this wild career choice. You will get valuable tools that you can apply immediately and try out in the beginning stages of building your own speaking and training practice.

Some people might call this a "how-to approach" to the speaking and training business. I like to think of it also as being a "what-to" approach: "What is it that I can bring to audiences that will touch hearts and change lives?" "What is stopping me from pursuing my dream as a professional speaker and trainer?" "What can I do to sharpen my skills as a presenter and develop my contacts for better speaking opportunities?" "What can I do to expose my programs to the international marketplace?" "What will it take for me to pursue this dream and what will it cost?" And finally, "What is calling me to this profession?"

Speaking and Training: Is It a Calling? . . . .

Every successful speaker/trainer I have ever known has a story to tell about attending a conference or seminar, or being part of a training session where the facilitator or presenter touched them in some profound way. Many actually describe the compelling feeling of being "called" to the platform or the training industry.

Perhaps there was a time when you sat in an audience and felt like that speaker spoke only to you. And in your head and heart you were thinking, "I can do that! I want to do that!" And when you left the auditorium perhaps you were saying to yourself, "I too will be on that stage someday. This is what I am being called to do with my life!" Can you remember who that dynamic speaker or trainer was who first motivated you to consider this profession? Maybe it was Dr. Wayne Dyer, Stephen Covey, Ken Blanchard, Zig Ziglar, or Pastor Rick Warren. Or maybe it was Suzie Humphreys, Maria Shriver, Lance Armstrong, Debbie Ford, Keith Harrell, Warren Buffett, Maya Angelou, Brian Tracy, Tony Robbins, Tony Alessandra, or Les Brown. It also could have been a great orator from history, like Dr. Martin Luther King Jr., Winston Churchill, John F. Kennedy, Margaret Thatcher, Eleanor Roosevelt, or Ronald Reagan. In any case, when you have the opportunity to hear great speakers, whether in person or captured on a DVD from years past, there is a likelihood that the experience will stir your spirit and awaken your desire to heed the call to the podium or stage.

What to Expect from this Book . . . .

My goal is to present to you in this book, in the most straight-forward manner I know, a four-part plan to become a successful speaker and trainer. The objective is not to tell you that you can make millions by simply reading this book. I know that would not be true. But it is true that I have kept this book real world and practical, basing it on my years of extensive experience speaking to audiences around the world in every professional speaking format and venue that exists. I continue to make my living in this marvelous arena, and now I am sharing it all with you.

Anne's Four-Part Plan to Success . . . .

In each of these sections, you will find practical methods, self-assessments, exercises, tips, and toolkits to help you move forward as a paid professional speaker and trainer.

Part One: Understand the Business of Professional
             Speaking: The Good, the Bad, and the Ugly
Part Two: Make Your Marketing Toolkit Sizzlin' Hot
Part Three: Travel the World *Free* as a Speaker and Trainer
Part Four: Step into the Spotlight

I'm convinced that this book will empower you with the necessary tools and compasses for navigating your individual approach to entering this field and enduring the life-changing opportunities that lie ahead. Not only will it give you the direction you need to investigate this extraordinary business, but it will help you to build your confidence, determine your talents and gifts, face your fears, and hence step up to the microphone!

Heartfelt thanks go to my husband, David, and daughter, Autumn, for always being there to greet me after every road trip and tell me I did a great job. To Betty and Gene Garrett, you are an inspiration that resonates in every page of this book and in my speaking career each and every day.

Anne Bruce
May 2008

INTRODUCTION

I gave my first paid speech in a big red barn in Toad Suck, Arkansas. I got paid $500 and, boy, was I happy. I'm pleased to say I've come a long way since that day I propped my handouts and notes, literally, on a haystack. To add more irony to that first paid professional engagement, you have to know that I am a New Yorker from the Bronx.

Toad Suck was about as far away from my world and reality as you can get. But that's the life of a speaker/trainer. We often find ourselves in places around the globe that are far removed from the world we call home. And how fortunate are we to be welcomed into the diverse and different worlds and cultures of others? Very! When a speaker is invited to step into and experience someone else's world—other people's lifestyles, industries, sociopolitical environments, professional associations, and so on—that speaker or trainer gets the opportunity to expand his or her map of the world and gain more insights for developing their own repertoire of speaking and training materials. In my opinion, it's the speaker/trainer who is the greatest beneficiary when this happens. Audiences will always give you more than you could ever give them.

What you as a presenter put out there is always going to be

reflected back to you in grander, more intense proportions, as you grow yourself and your platform of topics and product lines in years to come.

You Gotta Start Somewhere. . . . .

The reason I share with you my beginnings right up front is this— we all have to start somewhere. Whether it's Toad Suck, Arkansas, or Skunk City, New York (a west-side area in Syracuse), the word *podunk*, defined by the Merriam-Webster Collegiate Dictionary as a small unimportant and isolated town, may, indeed, be just where you start your speaking and training career. Never be ashamed of where you get your start.

And as any speaker in Podunk (and yes, there are real towns with this name) will testify to, in the twenty-first century, with the breakneck speed of the Internet matched up to ever-evolving mobile technology, like more sophisticated cell/video/camera phones, wireless computers and handhelds, iPods, interactive television, and much more, there's really no such thing as a small and unimportant town anywhere anymore. The residents of Podunk may just want to hear what you have to say, and be willing to pay you for it, after checking out your website and viewing your streaming online video.

Timid and Needy Need Not Apply . . . .

Stepping up to a microphone with 200 people in an auditorium waiting to hear what you have to say as you speak your truth is not for the faint of heart, the timid, the uninspired, the lazy, or the inarticulate. The saying goes, "The meek shall inherit the Earth, but they'll never book Las Vegas to speak before an audience of 1,500." And if you're looking for nothing but positive praise on evaluation sheets, being told that you're the most amazing speaker

Where the Heck Is Toad Suck?

Toad Suck is on the Arkansas River. Tradition there says that the town was named for riverboat men and gamblers who sucked up whiskey like toads. When used to describe a place, the word *suck* can refer to a salt lick or a channel of water.

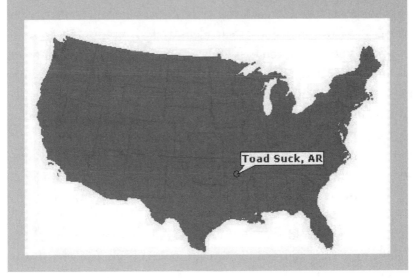

Toad Suck, AR

in the world, or if you require constant validation and adulation—get a puppy. You're probably not cut out for this profession.

Do You Make the Cut? . . . .

How do you know if you are truly cut out for this life in public speaking and training? I have come up with my own assessment tool to help you decide if this is really the right career choice for you.

Do you want to get into this profession for the right reasons? If the answer is yes, then you need to complete this exercise. I believe my assessment will help reveal your inner motivation for moving in this direction. It's not a scientific study, but having worked in the business for more than 15 years, I have clearly seen the common denominators among the most successful speakers and trainers worldwide and those who are headed to be chewed up and spit out in short order on the circuit.

There is one thing of which I am certain. There is a huge—and I mean huge—desire out there among people to want to be part of what appears to be an exclusive club of speakers and trainers who travel the globe and share their ideas and inspiration. I can honestly tell you that in the hundreds of presentations I have done, it is rare that I am not approached afterward by someone who wants to know how they can do what I do for a living. This is one of the reasons I decided to write this book. The interest in this field is extraordinarily high. And so is the failure rate.

It is my intention to help you to increase your chances of success and diminish your chances of failure. And the only way you can do this is to know the real-world working conditions of this business and then decide if it is worth it to you to jump in. I will give you real-world scenarios throughout this book. I took the leap a long time ago and have never looked back. It's what I was born to do, but it's not what everybody is born to do.

Stand or Fall? . . . .

Okay, you're thinking about chucking the status quo to jump into the speaker/trainer arena. You're pumped after seeing Tony Robbins in person, or on a jumbotron-size screen, at one of his world-renowned seminars, like *Unleash the Power Within*. You even walked on hot coals to prove you're primed and ready for anything. But now you're home and reality sets in. It's time to ask yourself, "What is driving me toward this profession?" "Do I know everything I need to know to make a go of it and succeed as a paid speaker and trainer?"

This exercise is not about having right or wrong answers. It's simply about helping you to reveal the reasons why you think you can make it in this industry. It's a tool to uncover your strengths and determination to make this dream a reality. It requires you to ask yourself smart questions to prepare you for this leap of faith. Will you stand and deliver or will you fall and disappoint? This exercise will be the first step in preparing yourself for success and opportunities you never thought possible in a career.

Don't overanalyze your answers. Respond from the heart—that's where a speaker's and trainer's best answers always come from. As you go on to read this book, revisit your responses and innermost thoughts about becoming a speaker or trainer. Answers to your questions will reveal themselves as you learn more details about starting your own speaking and training practice and implementing the four-part plan for success in this book.

Self-Assessment Toolkit: Do You Have What It Takes to Speak for a Living? . . . .

Smart Questions	Yes/No	Your Answer
Attitude, Ego, Self-Motivation, and Your Unique Personality		
Do you believe in the power of a positive attitude? How do you demonstrate it?		
Do you possess a positive physiology? Do you use attitude to get well and stay well?		
Are you willing to do whatever it takes to get started? Will you speak for no pay to get the experience? How many months or years are you willing to devote to breaking into the business? Set a goal, be specific.		

Smart Questions	Yes/No	Your Answer
Will it bother you when you discover other speakers and trainers are getting paid more money than you are at the same venue where you may be presenting?		
How will you develop your speaking skills? Are you willing to join Toastmasters, take a public speaking course, read a lot, hire a speaking coach, or pursue professional certification? Do you feel above these efforts?		
Are you willing to start out small and work your way up to larger engagements?		
Are you thick skinned? Can you handle blunt criticism from strangers? (Because you're going to get plenty!)		
Are you easily offended? Are you easily embarrassed, or highly sensitive to how others respond to you?		
What motivates you to want to be in front of people speaking and training, day in and day out?		
Do some people consider you a "high-maintenance" personality? Do you require a lot of stroking and praise?		
Do you accept that extreme physicality can be a big part of this job? Are you up for it?		
Are you a low maintenance traveler, or do you require a lot of things to be comfy when away from home?		

Do you require lots of sleep to catch up when you're in different time zones? Do you suffer from severe jet lag on a cross-country flight?		
Do you expect to be treated "special" because you are the speaker or trainer?		
Are you doing this to be famous and make a lot of money?		
Are you doing this to enrich the lives of others, first and foremost? What makes you think you can do this and make a living at it?		
On a scale of 1 to 10, with 10 being the highest rating, what is your energy level?		
Are you an action person, or a lot of talk? How long have you been talking about doing this kind of work? What will catapult you to actually do something about it now?		
Do you feel the need to have an office space, instead of just working from home? Do you think your speaking practice will impress your friends? (Trust me, they won't even understand what you do for a living. Everyone will think it's a hobby.)		
Are you worth whatever it's going to take to invest in this venture? How will you financially swing it?		
Are you fearful of traveling internationally? Are you fearful of travel in general?		
Are you judgmental of other cultures, or do you engage in and accept the differences in others?		

Smart Questions	Yes/No	Your Answer
Yes, men are from Mars and women are from Venus when it comes to communication and public persona. What planet are you from and how can you bring a universal approach on your topic to both sexes?		
What's your usual mood, and who cares? How will you overcome feeling out of sorts and never let your downside show? No whiners or martyrs allowed in this profession.		
Are you a risk taker?		
Do you display self-defeating behavior when you launch a new idea? How can you prevent this from recurring?		
What is your perception of yourself? What is the perception others have of you?		
Who are you? Describe your authentic self. Have you gotten this far by faking it or doing it?		
What do you want to achieve by starting your own speaking and training practice?		
What strategies and tools will you be using to develop your practice?		
Do you maintain a positive outlook on life?		
How will you keep yourself motivated in this role as speaker and trainer? How will you infuse motivation into others?		
How do you influence others on a daily basis? What's your definition of influence?		

Confidence and Self-Esteem		
How will you handle hecklers, drunken slurs, insults, and other indiscretions thrown at you? How will you refrain from punching someone out who's misbehaved and embarrassed you in front of the audience?		
On a scale of 1 to 10, with 10 being the highest rating, how do you rate your level of self-esteem?		
Do you believe in yourself and your amazing talents? What are your amazing talents?		
Do you believe you've got what it takes to match up to the pros on the circuit?		
Who intimidates you? Why? Will that type attitude or personality get in the way of your presentation if your client possesses those same traits?		
How do you feel about your appearance? Can you cut loose and feel good about how you look?		
How would you describe the impression you make on others when you walk into a room for the first time? Dynamic? Regal? Confident? Secure? Knowledgeable? Timid? Self-conscious? Boring? Arrogant? Friendly and approachable?		
What one-word description would you use regarding your persona?		

Smart Questions	Yes/No	Your Answer
Are you a nervous person? How does it show? Does your neck get red when you speak publicly? Do you get red blotches on your face, or chest area? Do your hands shake? Does your voice crack?		
How do you transform jittery feelings into positive energy to propel you forward and make you more powerful on stage?		
At what are you spectacular? Name one thing you do extraordinarily well. (Lesson: You can't be all things to all people.)		
What do you stand for?		
What's your credibility in the subject matter you plan to speak about or train on? How will your clients and audiences view your credibility? How can you pump up your credible status? School? Certification? Degree? Experience?		
Will you have something else to sell besides yourself at your presentations? Books? DVDs? CDs? Or other collateral materials?		
Do you constantly compare yourself to other speakers or trainers and then come away feeling small and insignificant?		
Do you look at other speakers and trainers and genuinely praise the great ones and try to learn lessons from the best in the business?		

How will you measure your success? How will you know when "You've got what it takes?" How will you keep improving?		
Are you confident enough to test the waters and ask for feedback from others about your style and effectiveness on stage? What will you do when you don't like what you are told?		
Family and Friends—Support and Encouragement		
Do you have strong family support or is there resistance to doing this job?		
Who are the people in your cheering gallery? Name names.		
Who are the people working against you or preventing you from entering this profession? Name names.		
What will it cost you and your family if you pursue this career full-time?		
Can you be happy speaking only on occasion or do you have a stronger calling?		
Can you afford to not make any money the first year or so?		
How many days a month is your family agreeable to your being gone traveling?		
Is your family enthusiastic and excited for you to embark on this venture?		
If you are a trainer for an organization, or seminar company, you may well be traveling more than in your own practice. Will that work for your family?		

Smart Questions	Yes/No	Your Answer
Who needs you around most? Kids, spouse, parent, others?		
If it is just you and your spouse, will you want your spouse to accompany you on trips? If yes, why? If no, why?		
How will your family handle your being gone so often?		
Is your desire to do this kind of work a plan to "escape" your life at home?		
How will you handle friends who resent your new profession and your success? (Trust me, this happens.)		
Where will you get your support and encouragement? From whom?		
Can you put the "what-ifs" behind you? What if I fail? What if I can't get my old job back? What if I run out of money?		
Your Talents and Professional Side		
What's the most exciting revenue-generating idea you've ever had? What did you do with that idea? What was the outcome?		
What's stopping you from becoming a paid speaker?		
Are you comfortable asking for money and negotiating fees?		

Are you comfortable with an agent or speaker bureau keeping 25–30 percent of your fees?		
What's your greatest asset as it relates to professional speaking and training?		
What do you do on stage that sets you apart from all the rest?		
Will you consider being an in-house trainer for an organization to gain experience?		
Do you consider yourself an original or a copycat in your industry? If you're an original, prove it.		
Do you do whatever it takes to get the job done? Or if it is acceptable, do you only do the bare minimum? When have you gone beyond the call of duty and loved every minute?		
What value-added components are you prepared to offer your clients and audiences?		
Do you get paralyzing stage fright? How do you handle it?		
What help will you require to set up a professional speaking and training practice? Accountant? Website designer? Administrative support? Housekeeper? Childcare? Adult daycare for a parent? Boarding for animals? House sitter?		
What is your greatest passion? What could you do seven days a week, day and night, and never tire of it?		

Smart Questions	Yes/No	Your Answer
How does your passion come through in your work? Explain.		
Are you a great communicator? How do you tell the world who you are by how you communicate with others, audiences, loved ones?		
Can you handle not knowing when the next gig will come along? How far out will you be comfortable booking engagements?		
Suppose there's another tragic event in the world, like a 9/11? How will you rebound from loss of business if it affects the geographic locations where you work?		
How are you at riding roller coasters—in your professional life, that is? This business has more ups and downs than the roller coaster at Coney Island.		
Is security a driving force for you to succeed?		
What are you willing to do to make this a reality?		
What is your story? What do you plan to tell the world?		
Are you a great storyteller? How do you know?		
How will you continue to upgrade yourself in this profession as time goes on?		

Have you ever been published on your subject of expertise?		
What speaker or trainer have you seen that you admire most?		
Are you good at infusing humor into your presentations?		
Are you naturally funny on stage or do you feel awkward about being funny?		
What tricks of the trade will you use to engage others and keep them interested?		
What journey will you take your audience on? What will they love about it most?		
Are you creative by nature? What's your *wow* factor when you present?		
What's your voice sound like? Will you require a speaking coach?		
Are you articulate and compelling when you speak?		
How do you handle change? Do you welcome change in your life?		
How will you make this endeavor a lasting legacy?		
How do you plan to win your audience over and bring them to their feet when you are finished speaking?		

Source: Adapted from the Anne Bruce Speaker Trainer Seminars' Self-Assessment Toolkit.

The Successful Don't Ask Why

Did you notice in the questionnaire you just completed that I did not ask you one single *why* question? That is because why questions are deadly for speakers. They create victims out of otherwise professional people. If you ask questions, such as *Why didn't I get that booking? Why does he get all the good speaking engagements? Why didn't I get hired as a trainer in our training department at work? Why hasn't the client asked me back again? Why didn't the audience look more engaged in what I had to say?*, all you will accomplish is to paint yourself as a victim of failure and you will not see the bigger picture. When a speaker or trainer asks why questions, they remain stuck. Asking why weakens your power to move forward in this dynamic and fast-paced career. It also fills your mind with emotions and blame—a lot of generic information—not a lot of wisdom. And wisdom is what you'll need in this business.

The objective is to unearth your inner wisdom and answers to questions that you already possess. You do this by asking *smart* questions, not why questions. For example, in my seminars I conduct on speaking and training effectively, if I ask someone "Why are you taking this workshop?" Almost everyone will reply with their inability to have launched a successful speaking and training practice up to this point. Their answers almost always have them looking backward, bringing more problems and frustrations about starting a speaking and training practice bubbling to the surface. But when I ask promising speakers, "What do you hope to gain by attending this workshop?" Okay, now we're cookin'! Inevitably this forces people to look forward and to anticipate the future. Seminar attendees often reply with,

- *To improve my presentation style and get more engagements next year*

- *To be on stage helping others and to live my dream as a successful public speaker*
- *To realize my greater potential as a trainer and then start my own training company.*

See what I mean? What a difference a word makes.

Now here's a tip for you: How much more powerful would your presentations become if you stopped asking your audience why questions?

This assessment should put you in the right frame of mind to go forward and read the rest of this book. If any of these questions made you not want to be in the business, then you've just saved yourself a lot of time. Remember, it's just as valuable to discover something is *not* right for you as it is to discover you have hit on the perfect match of your life. So what's it going to be? My gut tells me you're going forward and with gusto, or you would not have purchased this book and read this far in the first place.

Speaker, Know Thyself

Becoming a great speaker and trainer starts with self-awareness. Epictetus, the Greek philosopher and speaker from the early second century, taught lessons in ethics, happiness, and flourishing in one's life. It is his words that underscore the lesson to be learned in this introduction: "First say to yourself what you would be; and then do what you have to do."

PART ONE

Understand the Business of Professional Speaking: The Good, the Bad, and the Ugly

 **Chapter 1**

Speaking and Training for a Living: The Ups and Downs

Professional speaking and training is a phenomenal and exciting business to be in. I have loved it from day one and I think you will, too. That said, it is imperative that you understand just what you are getting yourself into. I've been an insider in this world for years, and I can tell you that the more you know going into it, the better your chances of experiencing success, personal satisfaction, and overall happiness.

This career can be both tremendously rewarding and tremendously disappointing at the same time. I'll explain: It's a roller coaster, pure and simple, and if you don't have the stomach for the sudden drops and sharp turns that are sure to happen on this crazy ride, then you may not be cut out for the speaking and training profession.

I want to point out the good, the bad, and the ugly of building a profitable speaking and training business in the 21st century. You already began assessing your desires and the talents required of someone in this career in the introduction to this book. That's when I asked that you take time to review and respond to the questions in the *So You Want to Be a Professional Speaker and Trainer* self-assessment toolkit.

Remember, your assignment was not to have all the answers, or even the right answers. The goal was to use the toolkit to start revealing within yourself your individual strengths and weaknesses, the hurdles you may face, and the real-world issues you could encounter along the way as a paid presenter. This self-assessment is offered in the introduction to help you establish a mindset for tackling the rest of the information in this book and then start moving your plan forward to build a profitable speaking and training business.

You've already examined and provided answers to the four critical parts of what it takes to succeed as a professional speaker and trainer. Let's review them here:

1. Attitude, Ego, Self-Motivation, and Your Unique Personality
2. Confidence and Self-Esteem—Support and Encouragement
3. Family and Friends
4. Your Talents and Professional Side.

Completing this exercise first is a good start. Now it's time to reveal the good, the bad, and the ugly of what it means to get hired to speak and train at a professional level and what is required to build a profitable speaking and training business.

The Good

This business is fun and that's *good!* A lot of professions are not fun. Whether you are on a stage speaking before an audience of

500 people at a sales meeting in Dallas, or facilitating a small group retreat for a dozen or fewer business executives in Palm Springs, standing before an audience giving your presentation really gets the adrenalin flowing and gets the endorphins to kick in. And that is very good.

Professional Speaking and Training Is Holistic

Having fun is a good ingredient to have in our careers, because having fun is actually holistic. Having fun and a good time while speaking and training stimulates the pituitary gland, which produces endorphins and enkephalins. These are pain killer equivalents that are 100 times more powerful than morphine. The deep-down good feelings you will get from speaking and training can have great physiological benefits that can actually make you healthier and keep you that way. And that's good.

Seldom in this business does boredom seep in, because there's nothing to be bored about. Every gig is different, every audience is unique, every client and industry becomes a learning experience.

The other good part about this kind of work is that you get to touch others' lives and influence people from all over the world. If you're really good at what you do, you'll travel for free—yes *free*—from Tennessee to Timbuktu. You'll experience and learn from wide and varied cultures you may have never dreamed you'd visit.

And here's another exciting spin-off and really good thing about being a speaker and trainer. You may get a book deal! That's right. Remember, as a paid speaker or trainer, you are the subject matter expert on your topic. Your speech or training program may well become the catalyst to becoming a bestselling author. And then guess what happens? From those published books, you get more speaking and training engagements. There are a lot of moving components to this business, and they all feed

Holistic Speaking and Training for a Living

Professional speaking and training opportunities often come about organically, evolving over time in a holistic and natural way. Evolving into a speaking career is based upon a cumulative repertoire of one's competencies, skills, experience, and education, which is then applied to a collection of a speaker's programs over time. The term for this is *portfolio speaking career.*

For example, Jeanine Finelli, certified health counselor, built a successful and holistic portfolio speaking and training practice in just this way. She followed her instincts and her passion for her clients' health and happiness and grew her speaking career with the right training and credentials. Finelli pursued certification as a health counselor from the Institute for Integrative Nutrition (IIN), a partnership program with the Teachers College at Columbia University.

"It was a combination of my continuous education and credentials, parlayed with my enormous desire to grow a holistic health counseling practice, that just naturally led me to speaking and consulting for a living at hospitals, in corporations, and among my personal clientele using one-on-one coaching techniques," says Finelli. Check out her Love Yourself to Health Program (www.jeaninefinelli.com) for a great example of how a person's desire to help others grew into a holistic and profitable speaking and consulting career.

Finelli Health Counselor

Your personalized program will radically improve your health and happiness. Together, we will explore concerns specific to you and your body and discover the tools you need for a lifetime of balance.

You Will...

- Set and accomplish goals
- Explore new foods
- Understand and reduce cravings
- Increase energy
- Feel better in your body
- Improve personal relationships

Jeanine Finelli
Health Counselor
Cary, North Carolina
(919) 680-2711
Contact Me

Food changes everything. As your daily diet changes, your body changes and your happiness improves. Imagine what your life would be like if you had clear thinking, energy and excitement every day.

Your Program includes...

- Two, one-hour sessions per month
- Group seminars and classes covering a variety of health-related topics
- E-mail support between sessions

Source: www.jeaninefinelli.com. Printed with permission.

into one another and create the synergy required to catapult you to speaker and trainer stardom.

The Bad . . . .

You may have heard of Harold S. Kushner's bestselling book *When Bad Things Happen to Good People*. In this business, like any other, *bad* things do happen and they can happen to anyone, even really good speakers and trainers.

Professional speakers and trainers are free agents. They work for themselves and they depend on being able to do the job in order to get paid. Frankly, no one cares if you're sick or if you're stuck in a blizzard at O'Hare International Airport. The client has 900 delegates flying in and they expect their keynote speaker or workshop leader to be there—no matter what.

I think this is the hardest part of this work. There is no calling in sick, or let's just say, it is rare. It's not like holding down a regular job where you have paid sick days or bereavement time off. In this business, if you don't speak, you don't get paid. If you don't conduct the training, you don't get paid. Hardly anyone talks about this side of the business. But it's the real deal and I am telling it to you now.

In more than 15 years, I've had only two times when I was simply too ill to work. Each time, it cost me thousands of dollars, plus I knew I'd disappointed a lot of attendees at both events. It's no wonder highly successful speakers, like Tony Alessandra, bestselling author of *The Platinum Rule*, always come through when it's show time.

I heard Tony Alessandra speak years ago at a National Speakers Association (NSA) presentation for up-and-coming speakers. His speech was awe inspiring on every level. I'll never forget when he referred to how the show must go on, even when a speaker is ill. He then told his own story of having a 105-degree fever and chills and still presenting as the headliner. He delivered the program and nearly collapsed when he got off the stage. No one ever knew how ill he was. But he knew he couldn't let his audience down, no matter what. I never forgot that story. The pressure can be tremendous in this business. That's why successful professional speakers have an amazing amount of fortitude and ability to rise above their own crises.

I once went on stage before hundreds of people to do an all-day workshop after receiving word that my husband was admitted to a hospital. Talk about being distracted. But as a professional speaker, I know how to re-focus on the spot when called for, even in the toughest times. That's when you weigh what to do next. In this case, because my husband assured me he was in the best of hands, I did the job and then took the red-eye home that night. A big part of sustainability in this business is always having a plan B for when bad things happen. That means being prepared for anything.

For example, my plan B includes that I have back-up trainers I can call in a heartbeat to take over my training sessions

Take a Bow: Tony Alessandra

Tony Alessandra was inducted into the NSA Hall of Fame in 1985. He began his professional speaking career while still a doctoral student in the late 1970s. Today Tony is a member of the Speaker's Roundtable—a prestigious group of 20 of the world's most recognized and sought-after professional speakers. At this writing, Tony's written 14 books that have been translated into 16 foreign languages and has an extensive collection of collateral materials he's developed and sells through his online bookstore and other online channels. He's even created an Affiliate Program where you can earn a commission every time someone purchases one of his products. For more information, visit TonyAlessandra.com.

in the event of an extreme emergency. These are people who know my programs, my style, and what my clients want. They are the perfect pinch hitters. Every professional presenter needs a back-up plan for every event. I also know how far I can push myself if I am not feeling well. I certainly don't want to get on stage and faint, but I know when I can keep going and keep up a good front. All good speakers know their limits when it comes to putting on a good appearance, even in the face of feeling lousy as hell.

The Cardinal Rule of Travel

Unforeseen situations can play a very bad part in your speaking career. So why take chances? I never fly into the city where I am speaking on the actual day of my presentation. Never. Even if I am to speak that afternoon, I will not fly in, drive, or take a train that morning. There simply are too many factors out of my control that can delay my arrival, like severe weather, an accident on the highway, a bomb scare at the airport, and many more things that make life's odd occurrences happen.

I learned this lesson the hard way, and now I always arrive the night before a presentation. That way, the next morning I am right there in the hotel where I am speaking, or in the city near the event ready to go. One way or the other, I will get to where my audience is waiting.

I do a lot of speaking and training in the Winston-Salem and Asheville areas of North Carolina. Both locations are only a four-hour drive from where I live, but I always arrive the night before my speaking. I also can tell you that my clients always appreciate that I am there and ready to go the evening before their big event! And remember, even a small event is a big event for the client.

Just remember, bad things really do happen to good speakers and trainers. And they can and eventually will happen to you, too. If you have a back-up plan, however, for your work and for your clients, you will have a much better chance of keeping a solid reputation for showing up, and you will be able to keep your momentum, even in tough times. And that's what the best-of-the-best speakers and trainers do—they keep moving forward.

The Ugly.

The ugly part of this industry is that there is fierce competition. You must be an extremely competitive person to survive and thrive. If you think you are the most compelling, entertaining, or humorous trainer out there, think again. There are probably dozens of trainers and presenters out there who do what you do, and probably better, and maybe even cheaper. He or she who gets the booking survives. This is a business, not a hobby or a game.

Another ugly part of this business is seeing people go out of business. Getting one paid engagement is not enough to sustain you and pay the bills. All sorts of unexpected things can happen that can quickly change the course of your entire career. For example, after the terrorist attacks on 9/11, every speaker, meeting planner, and speaker bureau owner I know was greatly affected, and not just for a week or two, but for years.

I watched several meeting planners and speaker bureaus go out of business within months, not to mention all of the speakers and trainers who lost so much work that it forced them out of the business as well. This was ugly indeed. Personally, it took me almost two full years to recover and to build back the business I had lost in a flash. Thank goodness I had a lot of work in the pipeline and several published books under my belt, which helped greatly. But it still stung, and stung badly.

Never Take Your Business for Granted

On 9/11, I personally lost more than $45,000 in bookings for that following six-week period. One of my bookings was to take place two weeks after 9/11 for a major financial institution one block off of Wall Street in New York City. I was to stay at the Marriott that was connected to the World Trade Center and is no longer standing. I saved my hotel confirmation number to remind me of how life and business can change so profoundly and suddenly and to never, ever take my bookings or my practice for granted. A business that you take years to create can all be gone in the blink of an eye. Mine almost was.

Of course, we know 9/11 affected the national as well as the international economy and businesses too numerous to list, but in this case, I am referring strictly to the professional speaking and training industry. It was a difficult time to be a professional speaker and trainer. It hit our industry particularly hard because so much fear had set in for the clients who pay us and pay our agents worldwide. Plus, no one wanted to fly. And this business is all about getting to wherever the engagement is, and that is rarely in your own backyard.

Create Your Own Abundance . . . .

I have discovered that for those speakers and trainers who are consistently successful at what they do, there seems to be what I call a cycle of abundance that surrounds them. It's not a cycle that happens accidentally—to the contrary. It's a cycle that is perpetuated by a speaker's or trainer's own ability to generate synergy in their lives and their businesses. This synergy comes from several things—their unstoppable energy, their consistent momentum in how they work, their genuine spirit that is audience centered at all times, and their magnetism in attracting loyal clients, meeting planners, speaker bureaus, and the support that comes from building relationships.

I know that there is no abracadabra or pixie dust to sprinkle when it comes to being successful. There isn't a rabbit's foot big enough to ensure that your engagement will be the hit of the conference. I've yet to uncover a special formula for success that can be duplicated. What I have uncovered is a cycle of abundance, and it is within this cycle, which we ourselves create, that we find the greatest opportunities for ongoing and continuous success in our hard-knocks business environment. Figure 1.1 conveys my personal experience within this cycle.

MAKING IT HAPPEN

Study this cycle of abundance. Make notes. Now ask yourself these questions:

- Where do I fit into this cycle of abundance?
- Do I attract abundance or do I attract deprivation?
- Who are the people I surround myself with? Are they the people who can help move me forward and give me genuine feedback?
- Have I shied away from competition in the past? Do I always try for what I believe to be a sure thing?
- Have I been using my most precious resources, time, and energy wisely?

There's a booming world market of paid speakers and trainers out there. If you're ready to join it, then you're ready to read on.

FIGURE 1.1. CYCLE OF ABUNDANT SPEAKING AND TRAINING

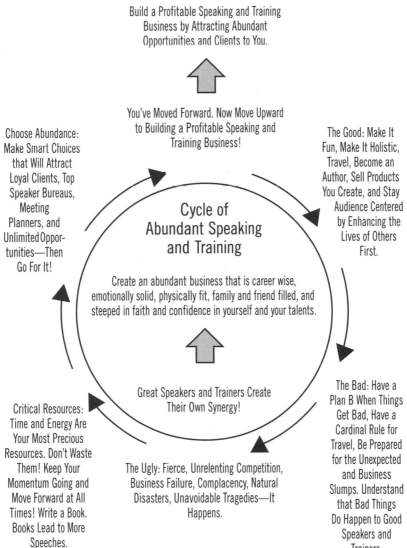

Build a Profitable Speaking and Training Business by Attracting Abundant Opportunities and Clients to You.

You've Moved Forward. Now Move Upward to Building a Profitable Speaking and Training Business!

Choose Abundance: Make Smart Choices that Will Attract Loyal Clients, Top Speaker Bureaus, Meeting Planners, and Unlimited Opportunities—Then Go For It!

The Good: Make It Fun, Make It Holistic, Travel, Become an Author, Sell Products You Create, and Stay Audience Centered by Enhancing the Lives of Others First.

Cycle of Abundant Speaking and Training

Create an abundant business that is career wise, emotionally solid, physically fit, family and friend filled, and steeped in faith and confidence in yourself and your talents.

Great Speakers and Trainers Create Their Own Synergy!

Critical Resources: Time and Energy Are Your Most Precious Resources. Don't Waste Them! Keep Your Momentum Going and Move Forward at All Times! Write a Book. Books Lead to More Speeches.

The Ugly: Fierce, Unrelenting Competition, Business Failure, Complacency, Natural Disasters, Unavoidable Tragedies—It Happens.

The Bad: Have a Plan B When Things Get Bad, Have a Cardinal Rule for Travel, Be Prepared for the Unexpected and Business Slumps. Understand that Bad Things Do Happen to Good Speakers and Trainers.

010810.62220

ASTD
(American Society
for Training & Development)
is a professional membership
association responsible for the
advancement of skills in the workplace. It is our challenge, our mission,
and our passion to develop professionals
to teach, train, and mentor others so
that the global workforce works
efficiently, productively, and with
inspiration. Through exceptional
learning and performance,
ASTD creates a world
that works better.

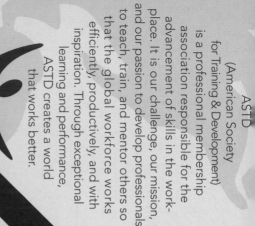

ASTD
WORKPLACE LEARNING & PERFORMANCE

Learn more about ASTD at
www.astd.org/remember

 **Chapter 2**

Making a Living as a
Professional Speaker

IN THIS CHAPTER. . . . .
- What defines a professional speaker
- Why creating a niche is important to your speaking career
- Tips and tools for striking it rich as a speaker
. . . .

There are hundreds of thousands of so-called professional speakers out there, but only a few thousand of us actually make a living at it. When I say make a living, I mean without holding down a day job or working the swing shift to make being called a professional speaker a reality.

How do you define professional speaker? A politician gives speeches. A flight attendant makes speeches about safety at 30,000 feet. Your server in a restaurant will make a brief speech on tonight's specials. Does that make all of these people professional speakers because they speak in public? Are there some other criteria for being labeled a professional speaker?

Here's my definition:

A professional speaker is someone who is paid to speak and then makes a living at it and any of its spin-off opportunities, like training and product sales.

If you're not getting paid for what you do, then it's a hobby.

That said, I want to remind you that I am strictly talking about the self-categorized professional speaker. I'm not talking about the emerging speaker who must practice before any audience he or she can get to sit still in order to sharpen and hone their style and delivery. When you're first starting out, money is not important. I used to give speeches to my cat Guido. It's only when you decide to make the leap and make this your sole profession that you've got to start thinking like a business person—making money is a big part of that mindset. Up to that point, you'll be in emerging-speaker mode and getting your act—literally—together.

Lorri Allen's Tips for the Emerging Speaker . . . .

When I first talked with Lorri Allen, it seemed like the phone lines crackled with her energetic attitude and vitality for this business. Here's a woman who's taken her passion for speaking not only to the podium, but to the training classroom, and now to Sirius Satellite Radio on *Mornings with Lorri and Larry*. Lorri's niche is speaking on and helping others make the cut as a profitable speaker and trainer. Her emphasis is on working with the media, and through her business, The Soundbite Coach (www.soundbite-coach.com), Lorri helps speakers craft their best message in media interviews.

Lorri's a pro and as a working journalist, she's not just giving advice from the podium, she's actually in the trenches doing what she espouses. Lorri's advice to the readers of this book: "Don't waste time." I asked her what she meant by that and she said, "When I started out most people would say, 'Oh you've got to do things this way, or that way,' neglecting that everyone has their own way." Lorri said this only wasted a lot of her time until she found her own speakers' groove. Good advice! See the sidebar for more of Lorri's tips, tools, and techniques.

Lorri Allen's Top Seven Tips for Emerging Speakers

1. *Join the National Speakers Association*—www.NSASpeaker.org. The information you learn at meetings and conventions will cut your learning curve by years. Plus, speakers refer other speakers for jobs. The networking in this association is phenomenal.
2. *Speak, speak, speak.* Don't worry about payment when you're starting out. Get the exposure and the experience.
3. *Learn from the best, but don't mimic them.* Watch the delivery (gestures, movement, voice, organization) of the industry's greats to know how high the bar is, but develop your own stories and style.
4. *Wait to invest big bucks.* Your focus may develop as you home in on your true expertise. Don't spend your entire marketing budget on products, DVD demos, a website, and one-sheets until you are positive you love your niche and you know there's a market for it.
5. *Realize there is more than one perfect business model.* The great thing about speaking is that we all get to success in our own way. Don't feel you have to do exactly what someone tells you to do.
6. *Implement efficient practices.* For instance, always be writing. The material you write may be for your blog or newsletter today and be stories for a speech or book tomorrow.
7. *Have fun!* Speaking is not a job. It's not even a career. It's a calling. You are going to make people's lives better by the words you speak and the advice you offer. Strangers will come up to you and tell you years later how you made a difference. Remember it's all about your audience, and you will succeed!

Printed with permission.

Let's say you've practiced and worked at this for a while. Here's more of my take on what a professional speaker is and does:

A professional speaker is someone who is paid for presenting helpful information to audiences, big and small, or to facilitate programs on his or her subject matter. A professional speaker has credibility worth paying for because he or she is a subject matter expert in a particular field. How the speaker becomes an expert varies greatly. Some earn PhDs and others go to prison, learn life's lessons the hard way, come out, and have a story to tell.

Some experts on the speaking platform have lived through unimaginable tragedy, like Laci Peterson's mother, Sharon Rocha, who writes on and speaks about her daughter's and grandson's tragic murders. Then there are those down-to-earth folks who can relay everyday life events, while possessing the natural gift of being humorous and bringing down the house with laughter. Erma Bombeck, the late author and humorist, was this kind of speaker. Many times, a professional speaker is a fantastic storyteller, someone who can grip and hold an audience's attention with their tall tale.

Treat It Like a Business . . . .

A professional speaker makes his or her primary living at consistently earning enough money to live on. Remember, running a business—including the speaking business—is about making money and clearing a profit after you have given your audience the best you have to offer.

For example, if you spend $500 to market yourself to a client and you only get paid a $100 honorarium, then you're sure to go out of business.

I am going to help you to better understand how you can make a living at being a professional speaker or trainer by investigating the many profiles of a speaker and understanding what a speaker earns in the marketplace. There are lots of ways to make this happen. I'm going to explain some of them here and more in the next chapter.

Create a Niche and Stick with It . . . .

The key to building a profitable speaking and training business is that you find your niche or your strength and focus on that area of speaking and training. I have built a solid practice on the personal and professional development of people and the higher understanding of human behavior in the workplace and at home. This is my focus. This is what I write books about. I don't do speeches on mobile technology or how to speak German. Those are not my areas of expertise.

Although they may try, speakers cannot be all things to all people. Do what you love and are really, really good at and the bookings will follow, as will the money. Heed my warning on this critical point. Do not attempt to be all things to all people. Find a niche and stick with it, especially when you are starting out. I see a lot of speakers, and trainers in particular, who try to be all things to all clients. It's simply impossible. Not only will you eventually disappoint your clients, you'll lose your credibility, damage your reputation, and wind up going back to your old job.

I had a discussion with Richard Boren, president of The Training Registry (see sidebar), who talked about the downfalls of how speakers and trainers stray from their niche when going after new business opportunities. "You might think that the speaker or trainer who offers a broad array of services is the most successful, but this is not the case," states Boren. "My subscribers who have well-defined niches are the ones who get the most business off of my site and do the best year in and year out."

Be a Subject Matter Expert, Not a Jack-of-All-Trades · · · · ·

Many clients clearly want to hire a speaker or trainer who is a subject matter expert, not a jack-of-all-trades. "It has become clear to me that when a subscriber responds specifically to what a company is asking for and then gives that company precisely what they need or want, that is the person who will get the business. But too many trainers just see the potential client as someone who might buy their 'other' seminars or services and so they try to sell those things without listening to and responding with exactly what the customer has requested," emphasizes Boren. "The trainers and speakers who don't have a niche and try to cover too many topics wind up going back to work in their original jobs when the market or economy gets tough. It's the subject matter experts who have the long-range success."

You Land the Deal, but Kill Your Reputation · · · · · · · · · · ·

I agree with Richard entirely. If there is one gem of insightful information you can take away from this book right now, it's get focused and stay focused on what you do best and sell that to clients. Forget the rest. When a potential client is asking you for a proposal, regurgitate back to them precisely what they are asking for. Don't try to market a program on supervisory skill building because back in 1995 you were a company supervisor for two years. That does *not* make you a subject matter expert.

What makes you a subject matter expert is a published book, long-term experience, credentials, certifications, and a track record for having success in a certain area. Trust me. If you try to sell programs to clients for which you are dismally qualified, you may indeed land the deal, but you will kill your reputation by the time it's all finished.

Training Registry

The Training Registry has been successfully matching speakers and trainers to corporate and government clients for 14 years. I find it an indispensable tool for generating revenue, and I recommend it to those of you just starting out as a highly valuable resource that can pay off handsomely if used correctly.

It is a subscription-based service that costs $139 for the first year; annual renewals cost $125. There is no cost for posting requests for any training services or products. The registry is a free resource for people trying to locate training and speaker-related products and services. Now put your business hat on. As a subscriber, if you get one booking—was this investment worth it? You bet. The Training Registry has been the most cost-effective marketing tool and investment I have made. I have earned anywhere from $35,000 to $50,000 a year in contracts that I've landed off this site. From this service, I've plugged into numerous multinational companies who have paid to bring me overseas for a variety of presentations on my books.

Visit www.trainingresgistry.com for more information.

Source: www.trainingregistry.com. Printed with Permission.

When Two Niches Are Better Than One. . . . .

Julie Wassom is known as *The Speaker Who Means Business.* Having known Julie for more than 25 years, I can attest to her slogan. Julie is president of the Julian Group, Inc., a highly respected sales and marketing firm with a specialty in child care marketing and education. This has been her primary niche. Julie exemplifies the power of subject matter expertise at work.

Julie effectively markets her own speaking and training practice, as well, on her website www.JulieWassom.com (see sidebar). By examining what the best-of-the-best speakers and trainers are doing, you can develop and create your own products, book ideas, and online e-letters and e-magazines. Julie's success as a speaker and trainer has not been limited to one niche. She's one of the gifted presenters who has successfully dovetailed her expertise in marketing to include another unique and passionate business—alpaca marketing.

Build Your Own Strike It Rich Toolkit. . . . .

I want to wrap up this chapter with a fast money-making toolkit on the practical use of proposals, and their content, and using them to focus on and sell your subject matter expertise to whomever is in the market for your information.

I like Mark Victor Hansen's quote about making money in this business: Find a niche, and strike it rich! This truly sums up the fastest and surest way for any speaker or trainer to build a profitable business.

I've used every one of these tools in the toolkit presented here and each of them have worked for me and helped me to make a good living in this profession. I'll never recommend that you do something I myself have not field-tested along the way. These tools will help you to align yourself with quality clients and customers who will be more than eager to pay you for your expertise.

The Speaking Engagement That Created a Spin-Off Niche

Source: www.JulieWassom.com. Printed with permission.

Here in my interview with Julie Wassom, she explains her shifting roles from national child care marketing expert to international subject matter expert in alpaca marketing. Notice that the common thread between both industries is her sales and marketing expertise.

ANNE: How did you get started as a speaker and workshop presenter in this unique industry of alpaca marketing? Did your marketing and sales background play a role?

JULIE: I was a featured speaker at the 1994 national conference of the Alpaca Owners & Breeders Association. In preparing for this presentation, I visited several alpaca farms and became enamored with the animals and cognizant of a niche I could serve in this industry, helping breeders market their farms and sell their alpaca livestock.

ANNE: What are your most popular topics for keynotes and workshops?

JULIE: Magnet Marketing—Drawing Alpaca Prospects to Your Farm Until They Buy; Contacts to Contracts—Converting

Farm Visits into Alpaca Sales; Cybersizzle—Effective Website and Email Marketing; and Keynote—The Squirrel Factor in Alpaca Sales Success.

ANNE: Do you do back-of-the-room sales after your presentations?

JULIE: Yes, my Alpaca Marketing Success Library of products and on-site consulting services are available before, during, and after my presentations.

ANNE: As a professional speaker and trainer, how do you make it easy for people to spend their money with you? How can people buy your products?

JULIE: At live presentations, online, by phone, fax, or regular mail, with cash or credit cards, depending upon the purchase method.

ANNE: Are your products made available at your events and online, or through a distributor, as well?

JULIE: They are available on a shopping cart on my website at http://www.juliewassom.com/alpacas%20order%20products.html. I do not use a distributor, although I do offer referral incentives and volume purchase savings.

ANNE: You've developed a strong and unique niche market for your services. What advice would you give someone starting out who wants to create a niche for their own speaking and training practice?

JULIE: As my friend, Mark Victor Hansen, says, "Find a niche and strike it rich!" I teach this concept and have used it myself to develop a niche in this and my other primary vertical industry:

- Investigate a specific segment of the industry where there is a need for your services and products.
- Determine what is unique about you, your products, and services.

- Establish an image message that communicates the benefits target audiences can gain from working with you.
- Use proven marketing methods and a layered approach to communicate your message to key target audiences.
- Use proven sales skills to convert inquiries into business.
- Request and nurture referrals from those who can broaden or deepen business in your niche.
- Follow up, follow up, follow up.
- Annually evaluate your niche, adjusting your services to respond to changes in your target industry.

ANNE: Do you supplement what you do with other speaking topics and workshops, or are you exclusively working in the alpaca industry?

JULIE: I am a speaker, trainer, consultant, and author in the alpaca industry and the early care and education industry. Although I have provided these services on a smaller scale in numerous other industries, these are my two primary vertical markets.

ANNE: As an insider in the professional speaker and trainer arena, what is your best advice to beginners wanting to start their own profitable speaking and training business?

JULIE: Get good at your craft. There are lots of speakers out there, but only a few who are superb. Get published. It lends credibility hard to get other ways. Get busy! The best one to promote you is *you*!

Tools for Striking It Rich

Decide what your niche is going to be. This is a speaker's and trainer's true north. Once you make this decision, you will have a built-in compass leading you in your most profitable direction. Be specific and focus on what you do best.

When you get clear on this, the money will follow. Think about the Mark Victor Hansen mantra and say to yourself, "I'm going to find a niche and strike it rich!"

Write down your niche here: _____

I am a subject matter expert on _____

Here's how I can prove it: _____

Get a hot topic and a hot title to support it. What's your topic? More important, what's the hot title you've chosen to support it? Think of a sample title you might use for your seminar, keynote speech, or training topic. Will it convey your expertise in this area and will it inspire others to want to hire you?

My speech or program title is: _____

Titles you select for your programs and speeches should be captivating, stimulate audience interest, and help you make money. They should demonstrate your creativity and energy, knowledge of cutting-edge information, and suggest there is something exciting to learn from the program. Your program titles are powerful marketing tools that tell the world what it is you are going to be speaking or training about.

Many times I've had people contact me about a booking, simply because they were intrigued by the title of one of my presentations. For example, three of my program titles based on my books on motivation continue to get rave reviews from audiences and generate lots of fresh leads domestically and internationally: *Motivating and Retaining Your Superstar Talent!*, *How to Motivate Every Employee!*, and

Tools for Striking It Rich

- Decide what your niche is going to be.
- Get a hot topic and a hot title to support it.
- Use Speaker Speedback to respond to inquiries within 24 hours—no exceptions.
- Have a detailed presentation outline of your program ready to go at a moment's notice.
- Create a template for every program you offer.
- Set your fees strategically and fully disclose them.
- Have a letter of agreement or service contract ready to be signed.

The Positively Outrageous Connection between Employee Motivation and Peak Performance! When an organization wants to offer a program on motivation to its employees and then comes across my website featuring these titles, they will often call and ask for my program outline and fees. That's one foot in the door that didn't exist prior to their seeing those titles. The titles alone are the grabber. Then I follow up with a detailed program outline and costs.

Examples of titles that wow, sell books, sell seminars, and sell speakers include Cynthia Heimel's self-help book *If You Can't Live Without Me, Why Aren't You Dead Yet?* and Betty Londergan's funny and frank *I'm Too Sexy for My Volvo: A Mom's Guide to Staying Fabulous.*

Use *Speaker Speedback* to respond to inquiries within 24 hours— no exceptions. I began using the term *speedback* years ago in my communications seminars because the word *feedback* didn't seem urgent or important enough. Speedback means exactly what it says, that you will respond within 24 hours to any inquiries, from anywhere in the world, about your programs and speeches.

Clients and speaker bureaus love it when a speaker responds quickly to their inquiries—the faster the better. We live in a world where instant gratification rules business decisions. Set yourself up with the latest mobile technology to be able to respond to clients instantaneously if possible, and at the latest, within 24 hours. My clients are all made aware up front that if they do not hear from me within six hours of their initial call or email, that I am en route and probably flying to an event, and that I will call them as soon as I reach my destination. And I always do.

I have to say that the most consistent comment I get from prospective clients, customers, meeting planners, and speaker bureau representatives is that I respond faster than anyone they know. Establishing my routine for speaker speedback with every person who contacts me tells them that I will deliver the same right-on-time, every time, performance if they hire me to speak at their conference. They know I will return calls and emails and get them whatever it is I promise in no time flat. Remember, time is money in any business. So how do you think this tool helps me to make money when I am pitching my Communications Excellence seminars and workshops? It helps me because I walk the talk. Would you want to hire someone to train your organization on communication skills if they didn't respond quickly and in detail to your questions? Responding with breakneck speed in a break-neck-speed world will get you more engagements and make you more money—fast.

Have a detailed presentation outline of your program ready to go at a moment's notice. I have outlines of all my speeches and training programs ready to go at any time I get an inquiry. Prospective clients and customers do not want to wait to know what's behind your intriguing topic title. Your title piqued their interest; now you've got to deliver. Have a detailed, bullet-point outline of your program, updated, and ready to send.

Create a template for every program you offer. Everyone has their own way to structure and deliver a proposal or response to a potential client about how they will deliver a training session or speech. This structure is your unique template. The design and the layout should be simple to follow and allow the reader to extrapolate items of interest—fast. Templates save time and help you to get information to your clients without delay; they should include

- your availability
- title of program
- detailed outline of the program's content with bullet points of what the program includes
- organizations you've delivered this program to in the past (give company names)
- anything that gives you additional credibility, that is, degrees, published books, speaking at the White House, overseas programs, or prestigious university, or association experience
- description of handouts or workbooks and who is responsible for duplicating them
- your value-added component to this program, such as giveaways and prizes, assessments, special handouts at no extra charge, and so on (Everyone's looking for a value-added component. What's yours?)
- length of program, times, breaks, and other logistics
- your updated bio, complete with credentials for doing this job (a photo on your bio is good, too—people like to see with whom they'll be working)
- equipment needed and other items you will require to conduct sessions, such as PowerPoint equipment, an LCD screen, a DVD or CD player, cordless lavaliere microphone or handheld microphone, whiteboard, a book signing table and cover for that table, and so on.

Set your fees strategically and fully disclose them. Fees are what they are. So put it out there. You'll get faster responses and more opportunity to make the short list of candidates being considered. *Do not* ask the client, "What is your budget for a speaker or trainer?" That is the kiss of death. When you ask this question, you look like an amateur.

If you want to be a pro in this business, then value what you do, set a price for services, and tell your clients this is how much money you will need to do the job. Of course you can negotiate at any point you deem it a good business decision to do so. But you don't start out by asking your client what he or she thinks they can pay. If you do, you'll appear weak and you most likely will not get the gig. If you negotiate with a client *after* you set your fees because it is a mutually agreeable business interaction, then you'll be coming from a position of greater strength and confidence. And clients want to deal with confident speakers and trainers, not wimps.

One of the biggest mistakes I see new speakers make is that they hem and haw about the price of their speeches and training sessions. If you do this, you will lose business.

Clients want to hear confidence in their speaker's or trainer's voice when it comes to discussing money. So sit down now and think about what you are going to charge for specific formats of your presentation. For example, what will you charge for a one-hour keynote address? A dinner speech? A half-day training session or a breakout session at a conference? What about a full-day or multiday program? What about follow-up coaching for workshop attendees? What about international engagements?

Decide what you are worth, what the market will bear, and what you must charge to stay in business. What is the value of your program? What is the value of your time? It's not about price. It's about value. If you are being booked by an agent or speaker bureau, then you've got to factor in their 20 percent or 25 percent commission rate. Write down your fees and review and revise them regularly.

And remember, fees are not some government secret that the CIA is protecting for our country's national security. Snap out of it and get over the fee disclosure thing. Set a fee and tell the customer up front. They'll appreciate that you're getting right to the point about money because you know what your program is worth.

Tell them what it's going to cost and include extraneous expenses in your response or proposal. Is your fee all-inclusive, or are expenses a separate line item? What about travel, hotel accommodations, per diem? Let's say your fee is $5,000 for a 90-minute program. Then you must add on your travel, hotel, meals, and so on. I like to direct bill my airfare, hotel, and car rental to the client and then charge a per diem of $150 for daily expenses like meals, faxes, airport parking, and gratuities, but this varies with every client. That's $150 per day, including travel days.

Be sure not to leave any expense out of your proposal. If you have to go back and ask for more money, it won't be looked upon favorably and you may well wind up absorbing the additional costs yourself.

Have a letter of agreement or service contract ready to be signed. I will cover the details of how to do this later in the book. But for now, understand that this is another template you will need to have ready to go and have signed by your client.

I find that most clients who hire speakers and trainers already have their own document in place and prefer to use it instead of yours. This is fine by me and it saves time. However, just be sure to read each document carefully and feel free to make appropriate changes right on the document and initial it. If there is something blatantly disturbing about your contract, then discuss it with the client. My experience is that almost every client or customer I work with wants to be fair and equitable with their speaker or trainer.

I had one client who used a contract for services agreement that indicated I could not speak in their metropolitan area of the state, up to a 250-mile radius, for up to 30 days after delivering my presentation to their association's members. This seemed quite inequitable to me because I make my living and depend on dovetailing programs in whatever areas of the world where I am speaking. I discussed it with the client before signing on and she was extremely cooperative. We agreed that I would not deliver any programs on the exact same topic I was delivering to her group to any of their association's direct competitors within a week of my presentation. However, I was free to deliver other program topics that I offer at any time and to whomever I chose. That made more sense and put my client at ease (that's all she wanted in the first place), and it gave me the satisfaction I, too, was looking for. I rewrote the paragraph as an amendment to the agreement and we both signed the document that day.

Most People Are Not Out to Rip Each Other Off . . . .

The bottom line with speaker agreements is that people who do not know one another just want to be sure that everyone is going to do what they say they will do and that there are no miscommunications on the day of the presentation. And there's nothing wrong with that.

For example, if a client gives me permission by phone to sell and sign my books following my speech, I am always sure to write that into the agreement. It's not that I think the client will change their mind or renege on their promise, but a lot can change over the months before the event takes place. For example, that person may leave the organization and forget to tell their replacement that I have permission to do a book signing, or someone at the top may have had a bad experience with an author who sold books after an event and so they are against ever doing it again. So for communications purposes, not because I think someone is out to get me, I make things very clear and do so in writing.

As you build trust and relationships with repeat clients, all of this gets lighter and easier to deal with. I have rarely found a client or organization that did not live up to their promises or pay me what I was owed when it was due. You will find most people who hire you are reputable and exemplify integrity. Trust me, 99.9 percent of the population does not wake up in the morning with the sole intent to rip off a speaker or trainer. And if something occurs that did not go as planned (and that, too, will eventually happen; it just won't be the norm), then chalk it up to experience and cross that client off your list. There are plenty of fish in the sea.

MAKING IT HAPPEN

- If you're not getting paid for what you do, then your speaking is a hobby.
- Find your niche and stick with it.
- Be honest and candid about your fees.
- Build trust in your speaker relationships; put agreements in writing to avoid discrepancies.

 **Chapter 3**

Wannabes to Celebrity Rock Stars: Many Aspire to Speak

Dying to Speak . . . .

Imagine how public speaking might have gotten its start. Go back to the Stone Age. There's a group of cavemen sitting around a fire one evening. Half of the men took part in a violent battle that happened earlier that day, first between a saber-tooth tiger and later a woolly rhinoceros. Suddenly one of the men leaps to his feet and begins communicating to the others what took place at the bloody scene. He starts jumping up and down making sounds so graphic and compelling, no one speaks or moves. He's acting out the battle, waving his arms and gesticulating in a way that everyone sitting in the group begins to re-live or "see" in their own minds what took place that day. The caveman is telling the story of what his group of hunters encountered that day and everyone is captivated and terrified all over again.

One caveman then communicates to another that this cave dweller is no ordinary man and that there is magic in his words. So the cavemen take the storyteller away and kill him. Today, that same guy would be paid a speaker's fee and probably have an agent.

This Isn't a Part-Time or Full-Time Job . . . .

Unlike other professions, speaking is not classified as a part-time or full-time job. Those terms just don't make sense in this profession. I may only give 30 speeches this year and conduct 10 training workshops, but still reach, or exceed, the income goals I set out to attain. Does that make me a part-time speaker or a person who does not speak full-time? Would I have to speak five days a week, all day long, all year long, to be considered a full-time speaker?

The point is this: This is a unique business where the terms *part-time* and *full-time* mean nothing. It's all about setting income goals and getting booked at the fee you want to earn so that you meet those goals. If you were to charge $15,000 per speech, a handful of those may be enough to pay all of your bills. If you charge $1,000 for a speech, you'd have to do a lot more speaking or other speaking-type jobs to survive. There are many and varied speaking-type jobs out there. It's not just about keynote presentations and training workshops. Having a good understanding of what the opportunities are in this business can best help an emerging new speaker to align him- or herself with various areas of public speaking and training.

I will say right here that 90 percent of us do more than one type of speaking. Yes, there are the speaking circuit superstars like former president Bill Clinton who command the podium and are paid well over $100,000 for a one-hour or less keynote. However, I assure you that Bill Clinton will not be running to the back of the room to handle product sales and then be heading over to the Eucalyptus Room to lead a breakout session. Celebrity speakers are in a different category altogether, and I'll explain more about those categories and their general fees shortly.

Different Speaker Profiles . . . .

In the meantime, here's what you can expect among the wide and varied jobs that come under the heading *speaker*. Which profile best suits you and your talents? How many of these profiles do you see overlapping with your abilities and willingness to participate? How do these speaker profiles fit into your fee schedule? At which venues can you make the most money? At which venues will you enjoy presenting the most? Make notes after each profile as to where you fit in.

Professional speakers and trainers are often categorized to meet the following delivery profiles. They are not, however, limited to these profiles.

Keynote Speaker

This is the headliner for a conference or large meeting. He or she is the star attraction who sets the theme or mood for the event. This is a featured spot at an event. A keynoter is often a celebrity or well-known author. Keynoters can be the kick-off speaker, luncheon speaker, or closing speaker. This person gives the main speech at a function. The speech can last 30 minutes to 90 minutes. Keynoters are expected to engage and motivate the audience.

Rock Star Platform Speaker

Tony Robbins is an amazing platform speaker. He's a rock star of the industry and that's a fact. He's larger than life on stage and uses bigger than life gestures while speaking. You have to have a larger-than-life presence and persona to deliver at this level. Platform speakers literally make presentations raised above their audience on a platform or stage. They know how to use headset microphones like Madonna uses in her act, and they know how to work with a highly professional audio visual team as they go about delivering their highly energetic and entertaining program. They move around the stage like gazelles and they never use notes or a podium or lectern. These speakers are in perpetual motion and are considered the rock stars of professional speaking.

Trainer

Trainers expressly create skill transfer among groups of 10 to 30 learners. They conduct workshops and seminars of varying length. Trainers who are independent contractors might offer mini-workshops or half-day workshops; some do full-day seminars; others do multiple-day training sessions. Trainers also can work for in-house training departments in organizations and corporate universities. They may work as employees or independent contractors for seminar companies, as well.

Facilitator

A facilitator's job and a trainer's job often overlap. Facilitators spearhead the success and learning of the group. Their job is to help their learners to do something better, such as communicate more effectively, resolve issues more efficiently, or learn to collaborate and become more constructive leaders. Top facilitators bring out the best in their learners by letting them do most of the talking and problem solving. Facilitators are experts at debriefing learning opportunities. They ask smart questions that get their participants thinking. They summarize and demonstrate what's taking place, and they often provoke intellectual debate and discussion.

Dinner Speaker

This form of presentation usually takes place right after dinner. It takes a real pro to deliver a dinner speech because the audience can be tough. They've not only knocked back a few, but after they eat, they get sleepy. Great dinner speakers are thick skinned and not easily insulted or distracted by boisterous jabs and jokes, drunks, or boring speeches by top executives prior to their speaking. Awards presentations are often the reason to have a dinner speaker. This can be lengthy and tiresome for attendees and so the dinner speaker must be able to jolt them back to the stage and keep their interest after a long day, a heavy meal, and wine with dinner.

Master of Ceremonies

A master of ceremonies—also known as an emcee, MC, or toast-master of a ceremony or banquet—connects the separate parts of a meeting or ceremony. He or she introduces other speakers and keeps the program flowing.

Moderator

This is someone who moderates a panel discussion and gives explanations of topics, rules, and procedures, and introduces panelists. A moderator also handles questions from the floor and is the timekeeper for panelists. Being a moderator requires keen attention to each speaker and audience participant, time, and flow of content.

General Session Presenter

A general session presenter addresses the entire audience at a convention or large meeting and usually does so within a two-hour timeframe.

Concurrent Presenter

Concurrent sessions are simultaneous. One is taking place at the same time others are taking place. A concurrent presenter typically has people who sign up for his or her workshop. These workshops take place at conferences and conventions where there are many workshops being held each day. Concurrent sessions can be brief, lasting only 45 minutes or so, or they can be half-day or all-day workshops.

Breakout Session Speaker

Meetings and conferences often have breakout sessions following the general session speaker's program. These breakouts can be as short as one hour or much longer. They offer depth and breadth to the overall subject matter or theme of the meeting or conference. Oftentimes breakout session speakers will include the general session speaker, who dovetails information from his or her key presentation with additional information on the subject. Authors often do breakouts and then stay to sell and sign books afterward.

Character Players

These professional speakers and thespians dress up like period figures, such as Abraham Lincoln, Mark Twain, or Rosa Parks. These presentations are big hits in schools and some businesses.

The presenters who do this type of speaking are knowledgeable and entertaining. They provide new and interesting ways to interpret books, famous people, and historical events. They are well choreographed and rehearsed to tie in famous speeches in history and historical roles that pertain to an organization's professional development.

Character players also come in the form of actors who role-play real-world situations in companies with specific issues, like coaching, communications, or conflict resolution. Each player takes on the part of one of the organization's staff and presents real-world scenarios and different ways they can play out in the workplace depending on how they are handled.

Humorists

Of all the speaker categories out there, this is by far the most difficult to pull off and the most entertaining eloquence to observe when done well. If you thought timing was everything in a straightforward keynote speech, try doing stand-up for Microsoft or Sony. These punch-line practitioners can range from Jay Leno, Jerry Seinfeld, and Ellen DeGeneres as heavy-hitter speakers at a convention in Las Vegas or New York, to lighter-weight humorists who show up anywhere on the agenda tying together inside information about the organization and leadership personalities to the event taking place. These funny-bone specialists of the platform can affect an audience well beyond the event where they create the laughter.

Show *Who* the Money? . . . .

With the exception of celebrity speakers, who get paid as much as $150,000 to an extraordinary $200,000 a speech, I would say the speakers making the most money are the independent contractor

Who's Booking the Stand-Ups?

Attention stand-up comics! There are tremendous speaking opportunities that exist outside traditional comedy clubs. It all happens on the professional speaking circuit. Humor is now the headliner at large corporate events. And who's booking? AT&T, Marriott Corporation, American Express, Bank of America, Frito-Lay, Inc., IBM, Kaiser Permanente, Coca-Cola, Pfizer, and lots of other organizations that want to bring a hilarious presentation style together with a meaningful message to audiences at their corporate event.

Stand-Ups Make the Big Bucks

Humorists are among some of the top-paid speakers on the circuit. And they deserve every dime. The fee range for top humorists is between $10,000 and $20,000 per speech, with the average fees running right around $12,000 to $15,000 per event, plus expenses. Not bad, eh? Especially when you consider all expenses and stays at beautiful resorts and four- and five-star hotels are paid for. It beats the heck out of working after-hour clubs and having cocktail peanuts tossed at you by the drunk guy in the front row.

Take a Bow!

If you think you've got the gift to deliver the punch lines that bring audiences to their feet, then study the masters of humor and start crafting your own knock-their-socks-off presentation.

Here's my pick of some of the best in the business. Visit their websites and take a look at their online videos, books, and event presentations. If you've got this kind of talent, timing, and tenacity—become a punch-line professional on the speaking circuit and live the dream of a lifetime. You'll make a heck of living doing it.

Examples of successful humorists include the following:

Steve Rizzo at www.steverizzo.com

I've seen Steve a few times and he is out-of-this-world great! Known as The Attitude Adjuster, Steve also is the author of the award-winning book *Becoming a Humor Being.* As president of Laugh It Off Productions, Steve speaks across the country using humorous principles that help audiences discover brighter alternatives to potentially negative situations.

Chris Bliss at www.chrisbliss.com

Here's what the *Washington Post* says about Chris Bliss: "If you're looking to laugh, you cannot do much better than Chris Bliss." And I couldn't agree more. His famous, world-class juggling finale has been seen by millions on YouTube—check it out. Chris Bliss delivers smart comedy and modern-day satire for the information age, topped with a guaranteed standing ovation.

Dale Irvin at www.daleirvin.com

If you don't think a corporate meeting can be funny, you haven't seen Dale Irvin. His clients run the gamut from Anheuser-Busch to Xerox. He's a humorist speaker and professional emcee. Visit Dale's website and click on his Little Shop of Humor where his books are featured, including *Laughter Doesn't Hurt, The Everything Toasts Book, Insurance as a Second Language,* and the *Lawyer's Joke Book.* His speeches include Laughter Doesn't Hurt, Five Minute Funnies, and the Corporate Challenge.

Ron Culberson at www.ronculberson.com

Ron Culberson injects humor into healthcare. With many years' experience in healthcare, Ron combines his knowledge in the business with the benefits of humor to redefine excellence for healthcare professionals. The result: improving the quality of patient care. Instead of consulting, he calls what he does in addition to professional speaking, *FUN*sulting! Among his presentations is This Won't Hurt a Bit: The Positive Side Effects of Humor. You can sign up at Ron's website for his free newsletter *Humoroids*.

Ken Futch at www.kenfutch.com

Ken Futch knows how to take life's situations and turn them into opportunities using humor and real-life examples! Ken's faced his own challenging times. For example, do you know anyone who's had a mule step on their head, been attacked by a crazed dog, had their nose flattened by a fisherman's paddle while water skiing, or accidentally shot himself in the head with his own gun? Ken has. In his new book *Take Your Best Shot*, Ken focuses on turning real-life scenarios into real-life opportunities, giving readers all the ammo they need to make life changes that aim them toward the top. Ken went from washing windshields to leading a combat platoon in Vietnam, to being a top revenue producer among AT&T salespeople, and now ranks internationally among the best humorist speaker professionals.

trainers. I say independent, because a corporate trainer's income is obviously restricted to salary. But a speaker who does speaking and training as his or her own business venture—well, the sky's the limit.

An independent contractor operates their own speaking and training business, like I've done for years, or they may work on behalf of a large seminar company, like Fred Pryor Seminars, or SkillPath Seminars, CareerTrack, the American Management Association (AMA), Achieve Global, or Dale Carnegie Training. These organizations, by the way, are great ways for trainers to get volume work and to build a following while sharpening their skill sets in front of an audience.

There's More to Speaking Than Meets the Eye . . . .

The professional speakers who also include training programs in their repertoire are the ones making the most money. I would say more than 90 percent of the speakers I know personally do training. And there's obviously a reason why that percentage is so high.

The biggest pay is earned in keynoting engagements—speakers who are a conference's main drawing card—the big names like Dr. Phil, Debbie Ford, Tom Brokaw, Deepak Chopra, and Ken Blanchard. But even Ken Blanchard's organization, The Blanchard Companies, offers hundreds of onsite training programs,

Revenue Potential Working with Seminar Companies

I've seen trainers earn $75,000 a year, and more with bonuses, working for a well-known and established seminar company as an independent contractor. However, these are all top-performing speakers and trainers, and several things hinge on their earning income at this level. Income relies on the number of programs they are willing to facilitate a year, willingness to travel wherever necessary to do the job, desirable experience they offer the seminar company, ability to think on one's feet and respond quickly to client and customer needs, and the ability to cross-sell and market that seminar company's training resources, such as other programs, books, and training materials.

There are seminar companies that typically pay their trainers between $500 and $1,500 a day, plus expenses, and so depending on the number of assignments that trainer takes on a year, their annual revenues can be quite low or quite high. Income you earn working as an independent contractor for a seminar company is really based on the volume of presentations you make and the venues and frequency of training programs offered by the seminar company throughout the year.

train-the-trainer sessions, and public seminars featuring their own speakers, as does the Chopra Center, which offers mind-body-spirit programs headed up by their own staff. And Debbie Ford transforms lives at retreats through coaching and in her highly popular workshops and training programs.

When I am referring to speakers who make the most money most of the time, or consistently, I am referring to the daily and ongoing business of *combined* professional speaking and training. It is through this combination of speaking engagements that you the speaker can achieve greater flexibility, earning potential, and creative blending of your subject matter expertise to a wider and more varied audience of clientele.

Seldom is speaking all that a successful speaker does. It's usually a combination of creating and selling products, writing books, a little coaching or consulting, and lots of training. And just because you are blending your talents does not mean that you have 14 different forms of expertise going on. Remember in chapter 2, I spoke about the critical importance of being a subject matter expert and finding your niche. The same applies here. You are simply matching venues and moneymaking opportunities to your specific expertise and niche.

Together, it's what pays the mortgage and puts food on the table.

Different Speakers, Different Fees. . . . .

Remember, the most successful speakers fill a variety of client needs and roles in the speaking world. The more needs you can fill for your customers while staying true to your subject matter, the more value-add you can offer everyone.

A keynoter may knock the socks off their audience with their speech on change in corporate America, but then that same speaker may be even more valuable to the client if he or she is will-

Four-Part Formula for Speaking Success

1. Select your venue.
2. Seek out the highest moneymaking opportunity for which you qualify.
3. Match venue and opportunity to your greatest talent strength, subject matter expertise, and niche.
4. Allow your ongoing preparation to meet each and every great opportunity that comes your way.

ing to offer a breakout session or concurrent session afterward to a group of attendees. Add to that a speaker who's willing to stay an extra hour, meet and greet their guests, and sign books. Now, suppose that same speaker brought along their fliers or one-sheets (more on this marketing tool and others later in the book) and was able to set up appointments for one-on-one coaching by phone the following week, while promoting their upcoming webinar? Now that's how a speaker makes money!

There are six speaking demographics that I've created for this book. The information is not scientific but comes from my experience and the confidential interviews I have conducted with speakers worldwide, their agents, speaker bureau owners, and meeting planners. Fees go up and down in accordance with the popularity of the speaker, the economy, and the economy's effect on corporate meetings and company budgets. What I've provided are general fee ranges. They are not meant to be interpreted as fact. Fees rise and fall with the times.

It should be understood that the fees here are *ranges* of pay that each category or demographic of speaker could charge or may be charging in general. Many speakers will price themselves at an affordable fee, rather than the going rate, in order to attract more business. If a speaker thinks he or she can do four workshops at

$5,000 a piece, or get paid $7,500 for one keynote, then that speaker may well shoot for volume discounts and earn more money doing it.

Volume work that is discounted is a common practice, and is something I do myself. If I am already in Buffalo, New York, I am happy to stay there for a week and do several programs and make more money in total than I would get for one larger fee for a one-hour keynote. If I am there anyway, I try to maximize my time and, therefore, my profitability. If I am going to be in a certain area, I will contact other clients nearby as well and let them know I am there and ask them if they would like to offer something to, let's say, their employees' management council one afternoon. Many times the answer is no, but then I've gotten a lot of yeses when the timing is right for all involved. That means more money for my time spent in that area. See how it works?

Volume Speaking vs. One-Time-Fee Formula

One Keynote Speech = $7,500

vs.

Four Workshops at $5,000 each = $20,000

Shift Happens . . . .

Professional speaking is a form of self-transformation that starts with a shift in your thinking and subsequently how you see yourself up there on a platform with a microphone, getting paid the big bucks to talk to people.

As a professional speaker and trainer I am certain of one thing—shift happens. I am referring to the shifting paradigms we speakers have of ourselves and of our confidence level in order to compete in this rough-and-tumble world of professional speaking and training. To survive and thrive in this business, you must be willing to shift your paradigms along the way so that you can earn more money and get better and better bookings. The key, however, is to shift up, not down.

The moment you decided to become a professional speaker and trainer, or to buy this book, you were in the process of making a paradigm shift for life. Remember, a paradigm is a way of thinking that becomes a pattern or model for something. A paradigm shift shapes the basis of a theory or belief in something—like your belief that you, too, can succeed as a professional speaker and get paid for it.

To be a part of this business, you've got to be willing to shift upward. It's all about getting better and sharpening and improving your presentation skills. When we shift our thinking about what we can do and how we will get it done, or how much money we can make, we shift our paradigms into a higher gear of greater potential, and that translates into greater success and more paid speaking (see Figure 3.1). To use a driving analogy, you can actually feel yourself rising to the higher road of professional speaker ability, while merging into your audience comfort zone along the way.

Keep in mind that there are inevitable pricing gaps between some categories because the ranges quoted from various confidential sources in the industry consistently shift over time.

Six Speaker Demographics and Their Fees . . . .

Wannabe Speakers

They do a lot of talking and they *want to be* (hence "wannabe") in the profession, but these folks are held back primarily by fear or lack of self-confidence. The wannabes never actually do much speaking, except perhaps at small community functions that they

FIGURE 3.1. SHIFT UP: 6 CRITICAL SPEAKER/TRAINER PARADIGMS

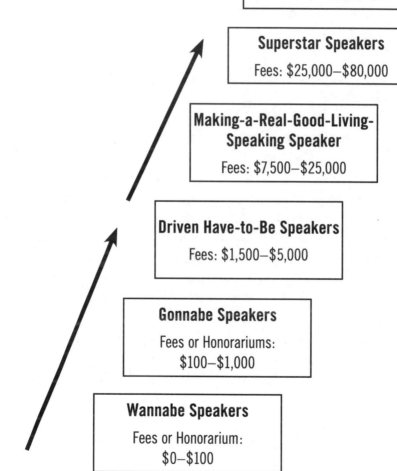

might be involved with, or when they make presentations at their homeowner's association. That's about it. Income from professional speaking in this demographic is zero to perhaps a $100 honorarium.

Gonnabe Speakers

This may be where you are now. *Gonnabes* are serious about getting into this profession and don't just talk about it. They actually do something to make it happen. They are the up-and-comers in the profession. They join Toastmasters, with an eye on the National Speakers Association, they subscribe to *Speaker* magazine, they get memberships in the American Society for Training and Development (ASTD), and they buy books like this one. They study the best in the business, and they practice, practice, and then practice some more, honing their speeches and then trying them out on friends and family.

Gonnabes know how to profit from no-fee presentations. They may do freebies for local organizations to get the exposure and experience but fully intend to get a paid offer along the way, and they do land paid speaking engagements that spin off from their freebies and the exposure they bring. Remember, even A-list comedians like Robin Williams and Jay Leno will try out new material at comedy clubs to test their audience's reaction. The gonnabes do the same thing. The gonnabes typically make honorium fees from about $100 to $500 per speech, and sometimes land a $1,000 event once a year. They are on the way to becoming the *driven have-to-bes.*

Driven Have-to-Be Speakers

These speakers are the driven ones of the pack. They feel something deep down inside that tells them that "they have to be" a success in this business. They are goal setters who are determined to make it happen, no matter what.

They are not only determined, but they are thick skinned. They can take the criticism and hard feedback. They have a business plan, and they study the best-of-the-best speakers out there. They don't mimic others; they adapt and modify other presenters' presentation skills to their own personality and unique delivery styles. The driven have-to-bes practice storytelling and, most of all, they invest in themselves.

The driven have-to-bes possess a good business sense about speaking. They know they cannot go far without the necessary marketing tools, like streaming videos, or press kits, four-color postcards and one sheets, and professionally designed websites and blogs. They spend their money to hire professional website designers; they don't try to do it themselves because they are focused on speaking. They invest in assessments and tools they can use in training, they get accredited if necessary, and they join professional organizations, like ASTD or Toastmasters International. They get professional coaching along the way. They do whatever it takes to make it in this business. They are the climbers, and they generally will start out making between $1,500 to $3,500 for a presentation; over time they begin to climb higher and then start earning about $3,500 to $5,000 per speech or workshop.

Making-a-Real-Good-Living-Speaking Speaker

The driven have-to-bes often graduate to this level once they reach that higher-level income bracket. These are well-networked speakers and trainers. They have built a reputation over the years. They have repeat business from clients and customers and have built a strong following. They may not be represented by the Harry Walker Agency, but they are most likely represented by several speaker bureaus across the country, and those bureaus are proud to feature them on their websites. They are contacted by meeting planners to present at meetings, and they are paid a decent fee for doing so. The range here in earnings is quite wide, and fees can generally run between $7,500 and $25,000 per speaking event.

Superstar Speakers

These are highly paid speakers and celebrities in their own right. They often make between $25,000 and $80,000 to speak at an event. At the low end they are well-regarded authors and professionals, perhaps doctors or former politicians, or famous business owners. On the high end, they are the Tony Robbinses, Dr. Phils, and Maria Shrivers. They, too, are represented by their own agents or top agencies and bureaus. Superstar speakers are often promoting new books or projects.

Celebrity Rock Star Speakers

I call them *celebrity rock star speakers* because they draw huge crowds and generate enormous excitement and adoration from their audiences. It's that same energy that you feel when you are at a rock concert and you can tell the audience is filled with excitement and anticipation about the performer about to take the stage. It's a similar feeling when the celebrity rock star speaker takes the stage.

These speakers typically come from major-name agencies and bureaus, such as the Washington Speakers Bureau in Washington, D.C., or the William Morris Talent and Literary Agency and the Harry Walker Agency in Manhattan. These bureaus book speakers, such as Christiane Amanpour, Bill Clinton, Michael Eisner, Al Gore, Colin Powell, Her Majesty Queen Noor of Jordan, and Bono. These agencies also book film and television celebrity speakers, such as Whoopi Goldberg, Bill Cosby, and Marie Osmond.

Speakers in this bracket typically make more than $85,000 in fees for one event and oftentimes $100,000 or higher, including first-class flights and accommodations, plus lots of extra perks. You define this demographic of speaker by the mere fact that their name recognition will draw substantially large audiences and create long-lasting buzz about an event. Events sell out when it is announced they are speaking.

What Are Your Aspirations? . . . .

I believe having this sliding scale of speaker categories gives us all a chance to measure where we are and determine how far we want to go in this business. Not every speaker wants to be a rock star and that's perfectly all right. Many of us do just fine flying at a slightly lower altitude.

As for myself, the most I've ever been paid for one single speech was $17,500, plus first-class expenses. The speech I gave was for a large insurance company. I haven't topped that fee for any one-hour presentation since. I've come close, but for the most part, I am happy to consistently remain in the making-a-real-good-living-speaking speaker category.

Fees are a very individual thing. But the one thing they are not is private. Once you are out there on the circuit, disclosing your fees is part of the business of staying in business. How you market yourself and your fees is of critical importance. More on this and how the best-of-the-best promote and market themselves wisely in part two.

MAKING IT HAPPEN

- Professional speaking isn't about full-time work, it's about defining and achieving your goals.
- Decide which kind of speaking you want to do, and what level of speaker you are.
- By including training programs in your repertoire, you'll increase your revenue potential.
- Successful speakers shift paradigms to earn more and get better bookings.

PART TWO

Make Your Marketing Toolkit Sizzlin' Hot!

 **Chapter 4**

If Your Website Is Boring, Then So Are You!

IN THIS CHAPTER . . . .
- Marketing yourself is vital to your success and survival
- Websites and blogs need to wow your readers
- Top speaker website picks from an expert
- Parts of a website a speaker can't do without

A speaker or trainer's marketing tools have got to be sizzlin' hot if he or she is going to build a profitable speaking and training business. Take it from this insider—you've got to spice things up if you want to keep up with the intense competition in this industry.

Now when I say spice things up, I don't mean make things look ridiculous. Your marketing materials should be first and foremost professional as well as entertaining and extremely interesting and timely. They are a direct reflection of you, and they tell your audience what they can expect from you as a presenter. If your website, marketing materials, video, and PR are boring—then so are you. Give creative flair to your marketing tools just as you would your platform speeches and training workshops. You tell the world what an amazing speaker you are by the ways you market and promote yourself. Develop your very own inventive signature style and then put it out there for everyone to see.

This chapter will be the first step in creating your own speaker and trainer marketing toolkit. In chapters 5 and 6, I'm going to give you more powerful speaker and trainer tips, tools, and techniques. By the end of part two, you will have your own mini-marketing toolkit, ready to power up and put to work selling and marketing *you!*

As you grow your professional speaking and training business, you will continue to improve, update, adapt, and modify most of your marketing materials. But we all have to start somewhere. This section of the book will give you the first steps to putting together an impressive and long-lasting approach to marketing yourself as a professional speaker and trainer.

Out of Sight, Out of Mind

You might well be the most dynamic and captivating speaker or trainer on the planet, but if no one has ever heard of you or knows how to find you, then who cares how great a presenter you are? The same goes for if you make your website difficult to navigate or if you fail to show people how they can contact and hire you. You'll never get an engagement because you'll be virtually unknown and never thought about. And in this business, out of sight truly is out of mind.

Successful speakers and trainers must have a ready-to-go marketing toolkit to build a profitable speaking and training business. To help you get started, I've compiled some of the best marketing tools, tips, and ideas that have helped me and countless colleagues of mine. These are ideas that have effectively promoted our speaking and training practices to paid engagements.

In my experience, an effective marketing toolkit all comes down to three important components:

1. Websites and blogs
2. Print materials and product lines
3. Public relations and publicity.

Create a Website That's Smokin' . . . .

A really hot website is as necessary for a great speaker or trainer as delectable French cooking is for a great French chef—one sells the other.

The key with any website is making it easy for visitors to navigate. Once you get someone to visit your site, you don't want them to leave until they've decided you are the best speaker or trainer to hire for their event. But you can't expect them to hang around if you frustrate the heck out of them.

Have you ever had that kind of frustrating, totally lost feeling or experience on a website? Maybe you went to a site with the specific desire to check out something and then buy it, but you got so frustrated trying to navigate the site or read print that was too small that you got distracted. So you said forget it, and you left the site for someone else's. That's what you don't want to happen when a potential client visits your site in need of a speaker or trainer for their organization. Yes, you can dazzle them, just don't make them angry while doing it.

Throughout this section I am going to refer to several pages on my own website, www.annebruce.com, as well as other websites that have brought me and my colleagues paid engagements over and over again. These references will give you lots to study and consider and will give you good ideas for your own site. Let's start by addressing the importance of having the *wow* factor associated with your website.

Blog Alert

Your blog doesn't have to be deep or long-winded. Short posts and musings that are relevant and worthwhile are what make a successful blog. Remember, less is more online. Short and succinct text is appreciated by website scanners who don't like to read long-drawn-out material.

What's Your *Wow* Factor?

What's your wow factor? Betty Garrett of Garrett Speakers International, Inc. (GSI) wants to know. And no one knows wow like Betty. "A great speaker or trainer has got to have that wow factor for me to even consider them," says Betty.

I've known Betty Garrett for more than a dozen years and she is truly the best in the business—candid, frank, concise, and she gets results. She and her company are highly respected worldwide by all who work with her. With Betty, there is only the platinum standard of excellence. Because of this, you get out there and you perform like you've never performed before.

So if Betty were to ask you right now what your personal wow factor is in the presentations you deliver, how would you answer? Stop right now and fill in the blanks, because without a wow factor, you just may not make it in this business.

My *wow* factor is _____

And here's how I'll prove it: _____

What's Your Wow Know-How?

You've seen by now that this isn't just a how-to book, but a *what-to-do* book. So I thought who better than Betty to help me show you what to do when it comes to designing a great website with a wow factor?

My goal is to demonstrate to you who's out there doing it right, how they are doing it, and then give you specific guidelines that will help you to study these examples, and in the process, begin creating your own website components with a solid wow factor all your own. So in her own words, Betty offers her amazing insights and reviews on her best website picks.

Do you know it's taken me a good chunk of my career to meet people at this level, share the platform with some of them, and land bookings as a speaker for a speaker bureau like GSI? And here you are getting to meet them and see their work, all right here in this book. What took me 15 years to get, you're getting in 15 minutes. So take full advantage of these resources.

Do You Know Betty?

Betty Garrett is the president and CEO of Garrett Speakers International, Inc., based in Irving, Texas. GSI is a highly regarded and prestigious full-service speaker bureau specializing in matching dynamic speakers to customized interactive presentations, workshop seminars, and corporate training events for its clients. Betty is a certified meeting planner and former president of Meeting Professionals International Dallas/Ft. Worth chapter. She is a recipient of the coveted *Marion Kershner Leadership Award* in 2006 and was named 2002 Meeting Partner of the Year by the National Speakers Association. Practicing what she espouses, Betty recently joined the speaking circuit launching her own professional speaking campaign and book tour as author of *Hiccups to Hospice: A Survival Guide for the Cancer Caregiver*, along with *The Caregiver's Companion*. Betty lives her passion by heading up both GSI and Caregivers4Cancer.com.

Your Homework

Your assignment is this. Go to each website and study what each speaker has done to make that website sizzle with their own wow factor. View online videos and see how professionally they are produced. Observe how each speaker uses his or her photos or illustrations to grab the viewer. Pay attention to the subtle details of how these pros so effectively market themselves.

Use the 13-point checklist in the sidebar to guide your review. Review these websites carefully and study how people who do this for a living are promoting themselves. Remember, the objective is never to copy another speaker's technique or approach, style, or speaking material. The idea is to gain insights on how each speaker or trainer comes up with his or her own signature style for marketing and selling what they do. You'll find that each speaker's website is completely different from everyone else's, but they are all equally compelling, entertaining, and fun to visit.

Anne's 13-point Checklist for Evaluating Speaker/Trainer Websites

Instructions: Make notes on what you like and what you don't like. List ideas that you can adapt and apply to your own website's development and creative flair.

1. **Desirability.** Is the speaker's home page inviting, or is it a turn off?

2. **Energy.** Is there "energy" in the design and layout of that speaker's website?

3. **Photos.** What kinds of photos are used on the speaker's homepage and other pages? Are they professional portraits or casual poses? Or a combination? Is the speaker in action?

Is his or her pose friendly and casual or uptight and formal? Ask yourself: Would I call this person? Determine the style of photographs you'll want to display on your site.

4. **Overall Appearance and First Impressions.** How do you think a website's overall appearance affects your ability to reach new clients? What impression is made the minute you arrive at a speaker's site? What "first" impression do you want to make on visitors to your website?

5. **Readability.** Is the website easy to read? For example, is the type too small or the background too dark or otherwise distracting? Are there too many artsy or moving/flashing elements that make it difficult to get to critical information? What sites make reading about the speaker fun and interesting? Why?

6. **Ease.** Is it easy to navigate from one page to another or do you have a hard time finding your way around? It should be easy and fun to visit a speaker's website, not a chore.

7. **Style and Sense.** What overall sense do you get about this speaker from their website? What comes to mind? Entertaining? Engaging? Professional? Confident? Boring? Strong stage presence? Weak stage presence?

8. **Products.** What can you buy from them to get to know them better? If there's a shopping cart feature, is it easy to use? If not, do they provide links to Amazon.com or other online retailers to facilitate check purchases of books and other products? How will you showcase your wares?

9. **Action!** Is there a video stream available? Was it easy to play and did it provide you with a sense of the speaker's style and stage presence? Did you like the person's energy and delivery of their material?

10. **Originiality.** What do you see that is the most clever part of this person's website? How will you be clever?

11. **Downloads.** Is there a bio you can download? Is there other downloadable, helpful info available, especially for a speaker bureau or meeting planner?

12. **Contact.** Is it easy to contact this person without answering a bunch of questions first? Can you just click on a contact button and get the info you need to reach that speaker and request their availability and fees?

13. **Creativity and Credibility.** Is there a "wow" factor—or a "snooze" factor? Is the website a template that is static and homogenized? Or is it original and different, showcasing that speaker's signature style? Is there credibility or questionability?

Betty's Best Website Picks . . . .

Following are some of the best websites of speakers Betty Garrett works with in the business. In her own words, she comments on each site as to why she likes what each speaker has done to build their wow factor.

When Betty first gave me the list, I immediately went to each and every website to investigate for myself. I learned so much from these amazing and talented speakers and trainers just by spending time on their websites, even though I've been in this business for a while myself. I'm confident that you, too, will gain valuable information, knowledge, and savvy insights to creating a great website just by studying Betty's Best shown in Figures 4.1–4.9.

Betty Says: Keith Harrell's website is one of my favorites. It shows his energy and has a great video. Everything is there for the meeting planner. It is clean, without a lot of "clutter." (Harrell is author of *Attitude Is Everything, An Attitude of Gratitude, The Attitude of Leadership*, and *Connect*.)

FIGURE 4.1. KEITH HARRELL'S WEBSITE

Source: www.KeithHarrell.com. Printed with permission.

FIGURE 4.2. AMANDA GORE'S WEBSITE

Source: www.AmandaGore.com. Printed with permission.

Betty Says: AmandaGore.com conveys Amanda's personality. Her video captures her energy and is easy to navigate. (Her amazing program topics include *Live Out Loud* (Part 1) and *Live Out Loud* (Part 2).

FIGURE 4.3. SAM GLENN'S WEBSITE

Source: www.SamGlenn.com. Printed with permission.

Betty Says: Sam Glenn's website is very colorful and shows great energy and action. (Glenn is author of *A Kick in the Attitude*.)

FIGURE 4.4. TIM DURKIN'S WEBSITE

Source: www.TimDurkin.com. Printed with permission.

Betty Says: Tim Durkin's site is very clean, but the one thing I love about it is his reading list. He updates this list on a continuing basis. (Durkin is author of *Moving Promise to Performance*.)

Betty Says: Linda Swindling.com is a pretty full website. At first it appears to overwhelm the reader, but it is easy to navigate. It has everything you could possibly want to know about her and her talent. (Linda Swindling is author of the *Passport* series of books, including *Get What You Want* and *Meet the Challenge.*)

FIGURE 4.5. LINDA SWINDLING'S WEBSITE

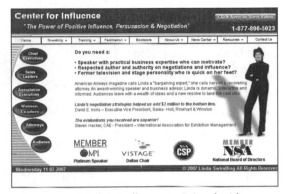

Source: www.LindaSwindling.com. Printed with permission.

FIGURE 4.6. CHRISTINE CASHEN'S WEBSITE

Source: www.ADynamicSpeaker.com. Printed with permission.

Betty Says: Christine Cashen's website reflects her personality. She has cleverly married technology to her website to make it very entertaining for the reader. I love her video streaming; it's so creative. (Cashen's DVD, *Get What You Want With What You've Got,* is available on her website.)

Betty Says: Joel Zeff draws the reader into his website. I think it has a great layout; it's easy to use. It, too, shows his personality and his talents. (Zeff is a national speaker and author of *Make the Right Choice: Creating a Positive, Innovative, and Productive Work Life.*)

FIGURE 4.7. JOEL ZEFF'S WEBSITE

Source: www.JoelZeff.com. Printed with permission.

FIGURE 4.8. BRIAN BIRO'S WEBSITE

Source: www.BrianBiro.com. Printed with permission.

Betty Says: Brian Biro's website has all the clicks at your fingertips. They are upfront and easy to navigate. His video streaming is short, leaving the reader wanting more. (Biro is author of *Getting Things Done* and the four-part CD collection, *Brian Biro's Breakthrough Stories.*)

FIGURE 4.9. JULIE ALEXANDER'S WEBSITE

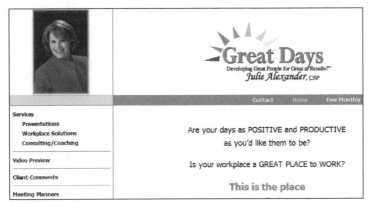

Source: www.JulieAlexander.com. Printed with permission.

Betty Says: Julie Alexander's website has a fresh, bright appeal to it. Plus, it is easy for the decision maker to navigate when searching for various items needed to make a decision. (Alexander, CSP, is author of *Great Days* and *Make Life Count,* along with her CDs *Maximizing Morale* and *Eight Ways to Great Days*).

The Common Denominators . . . .

Sure there are common denominators that all of us include on our websites to attract customers and market ourselves to our target audiences, such as the use of videos, or how we feature our books, the way we promote our seminars and training workshops, and the way each of us showcases our biographies and photos. Each and every one of us finds our own way to convey our uniqueness, talents, and personality. Each of us uses a style that best represents us as individuals and showcases what we have to offer in the speaking and training world. Our websites are a natural extension of who we are as people and personalities.

Here is a list of the most popular pages you will want to have on your own website. Go down the list and review each website suggestion and then compare these with what you find on Betty's Best list. Next, make notes on what you would like to include on your own website and how you will go about creating your own original style and wow factor.

Must Website-Have Pages

Homepage

This has got to sizzle. How will you make it easy for people to navigate from this point? Have your name out there—front and center—and all of your contact information. Have you written a book? Then have it on your homepage. Include a navigation bar that makes it easy for the viewer to scan the subject and select where they want to go next. Make it easy for people to get to know you.

Speeches, Workshops, and Coaching Page

On my site I have separate pages for my keynotes and training workshops. I also have listed separately special seminars that I do. For example, these may include seminars on how to get published and on topics specific to women. I also do life coaching, and so I have a separate page for that as well, where an individual can actually sign up for a one-on-one telephone coaching session with me whether he or she is in London or Lisbon. But all of these things are seen first on my homepage.

Products and Store Page

If you have something to sell, then you've got to feature it on your website. I do not sell books from my site, but I link my books to

Amazon.com for easy purchase. If you are selling your books on your site, along with other training materials like train-the-trainer programs, manuals, videos, DVDs, CDs, shirts, or other merchandise, then you'll need to have a shopping cart feature on your website, because now you will be setting up a virtual store.

Personal Profile and Bio Page

Be sure to keep your bio page updated. Use a good, professionally taken photo. Prospective clients can go to your website, print out your updated bio, and present it to a committee that day for consideration of your services at their next meeting or special event. Be sure you have contact information in your bio. Make it easy for people to find you. List contact information wherever it is appropriate so that someone can call you. Do not list your personal email address, home address, or your home phone number.

Rave Reviews Page

These are testimonials. As you gain more and more business, you will gain more and more testimonials. Always ask a satisfied customer for a testimonial letter. On my website, I list excerpts from client testimonials under my section called Rave Reviews. That way a customer can go to that page and not only read testimonials about the delivery of my programs but also see the various companies and organizations I have worked with. I like to have a nice mix of companies featured so that I have greater appeal to potential customers from all industries and countries.

Government Speaking Page

I have a separate page where I feature work I have done for government agencies. This is a specialty unto itself and so by setting it apart from the rest of the venues and clients, I am showcasing work I've done for The White House, the Pentagon, the CIA, and the FBI, NASA, and others.

International Speaking Page

You may not have a lot of international experience at first, but if you desire to get jobs overseas, then it's good to feature the countries where you have done work and have delivered your programs. I find this page is an attraction for multinational companies and draws a good deal of international business for me.

Speaker Bureau and Meeting Planner Page

I find some bureaus and meeting planners love this and others only look at the main parts of my website and do not care about a special page. It's your call. On this page you can include a list of your A/V equipment requirements, pre-event questionnaire (see Appendix B for a sample questionnaire), video of you on stage, and other items that can be easily downloaded for a bureau's client or meeting planner.

Press Room and Media Page

If you've been interviewed on major network television or in well-known newspapers and magazines, then you should set up a pressroom. On my site I call it Anne in the News. I feature interviews and articles I've done that pertain to my speaking topics. It may take some time to build enough material to have a pressroom on your site, but once you get a handful of interviews under your belt, it's time to set one up.

See You in Action Page

This is your online video. It's a must-have. This can be short, five minutes or so, and have clips from various presentations, or longer segments that feature you in one continuous presentation before a live audience. Your video must be entertaining and demonstrate audience participation and excitement, laughter, and applause.

Free Tips and Tools Page

On my website, I offer free articles, quizzes, tips, and tools, plus what I call Memorable Quotes. During my speeches, I will often invite my audience to visit my website for this free information and to take a look at one of my latest books. I have found that they do, indeed, check it out!

Blog Page

You'll find many of the website examples in this book also include blogs. Blog is short for weblog and gives speakers and trainers an opportunity to connect with the people they want to reach. Blogs allow speakers and trainers to share their passion and engage with clients and customers, speaker bureaus, and meeting planners.

Contact Page

Obviously this page tells a person how to get hold of you. In fact, you should have basic contact info on all the pages of your website. When the mood strikes, you want that customer to be able to send you an immediate email, or be able to pick up the phone and call you on the spot. Do not expect the person to answer a dozen different questions in order to contact you. This is not the place for forms. If you are trying to capture some basic information, just get the name and email address of the person and the reason for their inquiry. You can run people off in a hurry with a lot of questions or forms to complete if they just want to talk to you about an engagement or booking.

Hire a Professional Website Designer

If you think you can design your website yourself, you're most likely mistaken. Are you a speaker or a website designer? Very few people can do both well. Get yourself a top-notch website designer—I did! Elly Mixsell is president of Wired Communications and she's been my website designer for more than a dozen years (see Figure 4.10). My site stays current yet remains familiar and easy to use, all the while keeping its wow factor intact. If I can get a customer to go to my website, I know I have a good shot at getting their business. I asked Elly to put together a list of her own tips and suggestions for speakers and trainers looking to build a website. See sidebar for Elly's top ten tips.

Use Blogging to Your Advantage . . . .

As I mentioned earlier, blog is short for weblog. A speaker or trainer's blog can be anything from an online personal diary to a

FIGURE 4.10. WIRED COMMUNICATIONS WEBSITE

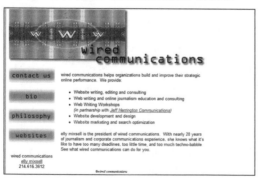

Source: www.wiredcommunications.com. Printed with permission.

Elly's Top Ten Tips for Speaker and Trainer Websites

1. Always put your contact information (phone and email) prominently on each page. You may not want to use your primary email account for this purpose, as you will receive spam in addition to valid leads. Create a specific email address to use for contacts from your website.

2. Research the latest technologies that are enhancing websites and evaluate their potential for return-on-investment.

3. Keep your site up-to-date!

4. Give your potential audience a reason to bookmark and come back to visit your site. Include industry-specific tips, links to resources, meaningful quotes, book lists, glossary of terms, white papers, tips, etc.

5. Feature books, media interviews, articles, and any material that positions you as an expert in your field.

6. Consider offering an email newsletter for potential clients to sign up for, but be sure the newsletter is timely and full of meaningful content, not just a sales pitch.

7. Be sure to include keywords in the code of your website to increase search engine visibility.

8. View your site on computers other than your own. You may be surprised to see how different it looks.

9. Always list your website address on all of your printed materials and other communication tools.

10. Add a media section to your site and include downloadable photos, bios, logos, etc.

Source: Elly Mixsell, Wired Commmunications, www.wiredcommunications.com

daily chat with fans. A blog is frequently updated and intended to interact with online visitors.

A blogger is someone who maintains and updates a blog, like a webmaster or web designer, or writer. A blogger may have a high level of technical knowledge or none at all.

Main Components to Include in a Blog

- Create a blog link on the homepage of your website.
- Choose a name for your blog—know your audience and who you are targeting.
- Create a content plan for launch of your blog—develop a presence with your first 15 or so blogs that you post, and start out scripting them before they are posted, just to get the hang of it.
- Plan a debut launch blog and create excitement about your blog.
- Include worthwhile content that is credible and timely and then continue to build your credibility over time—become the "go to" blog in your field.
- Include a dateline when you write each blog.
- Keep information short and interesting; don't write a dissertation.
- Use blog etiquette: be civil, be professional, play nice, and don't bad-mouth competitors.
- Invite response and be thick skinned when you get it.
- Make blogging fun.
- Include archives of past blogs.

Great Blog Examples to Check Out

A lot of Betty's Best picks for top-notch websites also included blogs. Here are two more examples to take a look at. I strongly

FIGURE 4.11. DAN JANAL'S BLOG

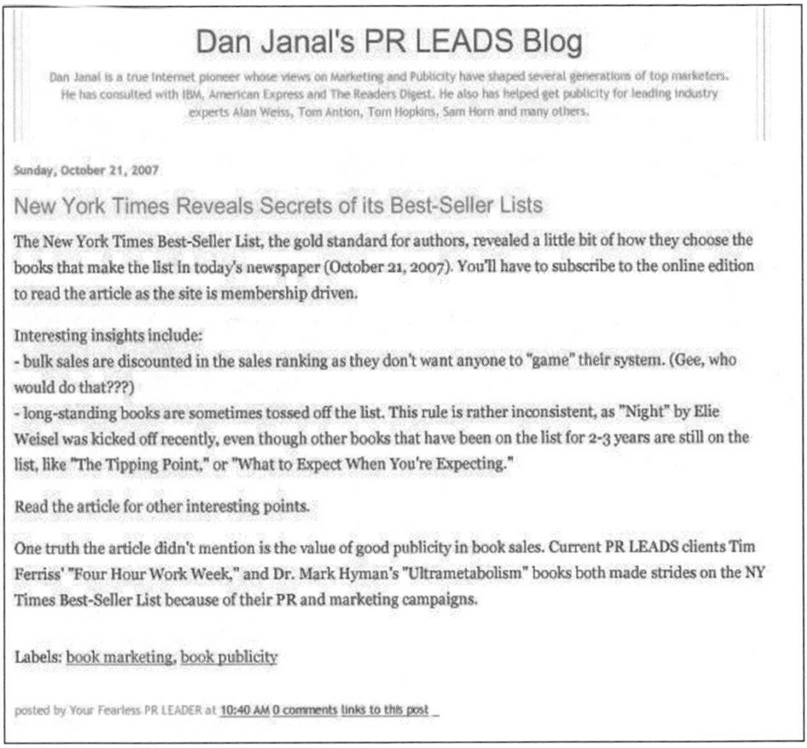

Dan Janal's PR LEADS Blog

Dan Janal is a true Internet pioneer whose views on Marketing and Publicity have shaped several generations of top marketers. He has consulted with IBM, American Express and The Readers Digest. He also has helped get publicity for leading industry experts Alan Weiss, Tom Antion, Tom Hopkins, Sam Horn and many others.

Sunday, October 21, 2007

New York Times Reveals Secrets of its Best-Seller Lists

The New York Times Best-Seller List, the gold standard for authors, revealed a little bit of how they choose the books that make the list in today's newspaper (October 21, 2007). You'll have to subscribe to the online edition to read the article as the site is membership driven.

Interesting insights include:
- bulk sales are discounted in the sales ranking as they don't want anyone to "game" their system. (Gee, who would do that???)
- long-standing books are sometimes tossed off the list. This rule is rather inconsistent, as "Night" by Elie Weisel was kicked off recently, even though other books that have been on the list for 2-3 years are still on the list, like "The Tipping Point," or "What to Expect When You're Expecting."

Read the article for other interesting points.

One truth the article didn't mention is the value of good publicity in book sales. Current PR LEADS clients Tim Ferriss' "Four Hour Work Week," and Dr. Mark Hyman's "Ultrametabolism" books both made strides on the NY Times Best-Seller List because of their PR and marketing campaigns.

Labels: book marketing, book publicity

posted by Your Fearless PR LEADER at 10:40 AM 0 comments links to this post

Source: www.PRleads.com. Printed with permission.

recommend Dan Janal's PR Leads Blog (see Figure 4.11), because he is such a well-known Internet pioneer in publicity and marketing. You'll be reading more from me on Dan and his incredible services in chapter 6. For now, check out Dan's blog, which you can access from his website at www.PRleads.com.

Another high-quality blog comes from media expert Lorri Allen, who gave you her top seven tips for emerging speakers in chapter 2. Go to Lorri's website at www.LorriAllen.com and click on Visit Lorri's News Blog; it will take you to her fun-to-read *Soundbites— Making Sense of the News* blog page (see Figure 4.12).

Why Blog?

Blogging has become a much-accepted pop-culture way to chat with your audience, plus it's easy to do. There are lots of companies out there who can post your blog, maintain it, and keep it fun. A blog can be a cost-effective alternative to lots of other marketing tools, or a great addition to them. A blog never goes stale.

With a blog you can interact with your audience and tell the story of your life, your business, or your speaking and training career. Blogs can get you noticed and enable you to engage your audience well beyond the marketing copy on your website. There are videoblogs, photoblogs, podcast blogs, and memoir blogs.

Blogs can make it easy to have ongoing conversations with your audience, helping you and your website to become even more wildly popular and intriguing to visitors around the globe. Blogs can be powerful income producers, as well, by including relevant advertising; you control how much and what advertising you want to showcase.

Blogs are mobile, too. With today's mobile technology, you can post your blog anywhere, including on mobile phones and on other tools using powerful posting and editing features that are now available.

Managing and Enhancing Your Online Presence. . . . .

Everyday there are more and more exceptionally tuned publishing systems out there for helping speakers and trainers, authors, and business people to better manage and enhance their websites and blogs. And there are lots of good website enhancers and optimizers out there you can research to fit your best needs. My experience recently with the website enhancement firm Mainstreethost .com was a very good one. Did you know that half of the people in the United States access the Internet every day? So as a speaker and trainer, having your presence known on the web is more important than ever, and now it's easier and more affordable as well. I advise researching and checking into these services every year or so once you get your website up and running.

It's important to say here that I normally would have had Elly, my website designer, handle this for me, but it was a matter of making the best use of her time and resources combined with the

FIGURE 4.12. LORRI ALLEN'S NEWS BLOG

Soundbites

Making Sense of the News

Saturday, October 20, 2007

Don't Give Up

This year, I have been a full-time coach and speaker and a part-time radio host. I only spend a few hours a day at that job. I tell you that because there are probably other interviewers like me. You, as a prospective newsmaker or guest, are anxious to get booked or hear back from your publicist and you probably think, "Those lazy journalists! Why can't they decide if they want me sooner?"

So that you won't feel rejected or passed over... sometimes it just takes longer for us to get through the stacks of books, letters, emails and phone calls. I might book an author who sent me a book six months ago.

Here are ideas to get you to the top of the stack:

1. Call when we're there. Remember that *morning* programs likely have staff that work in the morning.

2. If you can find a mutual friend who can genuinely recommend you as a great fit, that helps. When we're trying to find a guest, an endorsement from someone we trust can make a difference.

3. Send an email and make a phone call. I work in an old building with unreliable connections, and the email spam filter is confining. Don't count on the fact that we get your emails.

4. Be persistent, but not pushy. Nothing turns reporters off more than someone who doesn't get the message. If the reporter does not show any interest or says "it's not a fit," move on. If the reporter asks for more information or asks you to call back in a few weeks or months, she's interested. Stay in touch.

Posted by Lorri at 12:40 PM   comments

Labels: Publicity

Wednesday, October 10, 2007

Press Conferences

Source: www.LorriAllen.com. Printed with permission.

cost-effectiveness of hiring a larger search engine optimization company to just take care of my needs within in a couple of days. This way Elly was able to keep working on our current projects and I could still hire Mainstreethost.com to do all of my website enhancing and optimization work. It was a good team effort.

Any search engine marketing and optimization company you work with is there to meet the individual needs of your business. Primarily you'll want to get listed with the big search engines, like Google, Yahoo!, MSN, America Online, alltheweb, WebCrawler, and others. Next you'll want to optimize your listing with these search engines by selecting key words that, when typed into their search engine, will more likely pull up your name and business. This is why they call it enhancement or optimization.

There are lots more things a search engine marketing organization like this can do to help speakers and trainers:

- Website optimization and enhancement
- Website hosting
- Pay-per-click management
- E-commerce shopping cart solutions
- Reciprocal links management
- Traffic analyses of your website
- Email defense systems
- Website and form hosting
- Internet marketing, development, and consulting services.

No matter what team you choose to hire to help you with this effort, know that search engine marketing and optimization is no longer an option for speakers and trainers; it's a necessity.

There are many premiere professional blogging services for hosting websites and blogs that you can research. Check out Squarespace at www.squarespace.com, and visit TypePad, at www.typepad.com for starters.

This business of website structuring and blog structuring has become quite intuitive, so you need to do your homework and be sure that you are matching your website and blogging styles and needs with the right company.

You Get One Chance to Make a First Impression . . . .

The greatest lesson you can take away from this chapter is this: You never get a second chance to make a first impression.

Your website is without a doubt one of your strongest selling points for your services and talents. The effect and impression it can create in an instant is more valuable than all the printed brochures you can buy. Your website communicates to the world who you are and what you do better than anyone else. It tells the world that you are a formidable force in the speaking and training arena.

Don't skimp when it comes to getting your website designed and built. Use this chapter as your field guide to getting the job started and off on the right foot. Use the 13-point checklist offered earlier in this chapter to be sure you are including in your website the components that will undoubtedly give you the wow factor you need to make it in this business. Without it, visitors to your site won't be saying "Wow!" They'll be saying, "What?"

MAKING IT HAPPEN

- Know your "wow" factor.
- Give creative flair to your marketing tools just as you would your platform speeches and training workshops.
- Hire a pro to create, manage, and enhance an engaging and navigable website to attract business.
- Blog effectively and appropriately.

 **Chapter 5**

Five Ways to Double or Triple Your Income

The second part to creating a speaker/trainer marketing toolkit is to create products that you can sell and develop, along with the materials that support those products. The end result is called passive income and can double or even triple your income.

If you go back to chapter 4 and reference Betty's Best website picks, you will find lots of great product examples and marketing materials on each of the websites. I will get right to what I consider the most important things when developing product lines and other materials. These ideas can greatly increase your income and continue to serve your customers long after your training session or speech has ended.

In this chapter, I will be covering the predominant ways that speakers and trainers continue to market and sell themselves after leaving the platform or classroom. Notice I said *after* leaving the platform or the classroom. Whenever a client or meeting planner says to me, "We had a very bad experience with a speaker last year promoting and selling their products during their presentation," I just cringe.

How to Be Sleazy and Unprofessional . . . .

You know the old saying, "It's not what you say, but how you say it"? Well, in the speaking and training business it's both—it is what you say *and* how you say it. In other words, speakers and trainers are intelligent people. They know right from wrong, and it is wrong and unprofessional to hawk your wares in front of your audience.

I do not sell my books or coaching services while I am speaking. In the introduction to my presentation, I have the person introducing me say that after class or my speech, I will be in the back of the room to sign books and answer questions. But it is not me who is saying this, it is the person representing the organization. That's called a third-party endorsement.

The audience is smart enough to figure out that I am staying to sell products and also to answer questions and meet and greet folks. They certainly don't need to be reminded by me throughout my presentation that I have more to sell. As a result of how I handle this matter, I am always invited back to sell my products after a presentation. This is because the client and meeting planner know that I will not abuse the professionalism of the event or lower its prestige by making some sleazy sales pitch. And because I always write my own introductions for my clients, I certainly include highlights of new book releases, awards received, or coaching and webinars that I offer on a specific topic. I want to emphasize here a very strong marketing tool you should be using wisely—your speaker introduction (see Prepare Your Own Intros).

Appropriate and Professional Ways to Sell Your Products...

Having said my piece about hawking products and services from the platform, I will also say this: Having additional products and materials available before and after a program, for those who are interested, is a legitimate objective for any speaker.

Whether you are speaking to a *Fortune 500* company or a pro bono group, you can rest assured that there will be people in attendance who will want to continue growing themselves and gaining more education beyond your presentation, and want to do so with your materials and products. There will be people who are excited after hearing you speak and don't want to wait to order

Prepare Your Own Intros

Never let someone else write your introduction, or glean an intro from your bio. This is your only chance to craft your introduction and take control of how you are going to be perceived right from the top. Offer to your clients a prepared introduction that you write for them and let them know you are happy with any changes they may want to make. Trust me. Every single person that has ever introduced me at a training event or conference was more than happy to use the prepared intro I provided for them. It takes the stress off of that person to have to write something they hope you will be flattered by, and it is one less thing for them to worry about. Plus, as the speaker or trainer, you get the introduction that accurately describes your accomplishments, your topic, and what audience members can expect from your upcoming presentation. You'll be framed in a professional and exciting way that will move people before you even get started talking.

your products or books online. They'll want to buy them right there. I also find many people who really enjoy buying a book or product for a friend or co-worker and then having me autograph it to that person, which makes the product even more special for the recipient. You've got to remain audience centered when it comes to product sales.

Everyone Benefits from Product Sales

The point is this: As a speaker and trainer, you are in the information business. As your body of knowledge grows over time, so will your product lines. When done correctly, products and their offshoots will be helpful reminders that will leave a trail for your clients that they can follow back to you for years to come. It will most likely include referrals along the way.

The sales and marketing of your products and other promotional materials, or collateral as it's sometimes called, are not only a benefit to you as the speaker, but also they are a benefit to your clients and audience. The popularity of your speaker and trainer products does more than boost your income. Products and promotional materials with sizzle add credibility and prestige to you as a subject matter expert, and by doing so, they are a direct reflection on your client's choice in selecting you and your products to offer their conference's attendees or employees. When you present yourself and your materials in a professional manner, you present a professional image for your client, as well as the speaker bureau or meeting planner who booked you. It's a win-win for everyone.

For years studies have shown that your audience will most likely retain 10 percent or less of your total presentation. Have you ever attended an event and said afterward, "I wish I had a copy of that speech?" Buying your products will give your audience a chance to do just that and help them to retain the information you have given them. In the business of providing information, a speaker has the opportunity again and again to help audiences continue the learning process on the job, at home, while working out at the gym, jogging, or while driving. It's continuous learning in motion.

Professional Products Take Time to Develop

I am going to share with you in this chapter how you, too, can create professional and affordable product lines and supporting materials. But you must be patient. It takes time, not to mention money, to create and develop marketing products and materials of a professional nature. There's no time like the present to start planning for how you will incorporate some or all of these marketing methods over time. This should become part of your speaker/trainer business plan. Investing in your business with the appropriate marketing tools will pay dividends over time.

Your Homework

Remember to review all of Betty's Best picks from chapter 4. Go to each speaker's and trainer's online store, view their product sales, and take a look at other materials available, such as e-letters, e-zines, merchandise, and so on. Make notes and then continue reading.

Five Real-World Speaker and Trainer Marketing Scenarios . .

Here are my personal experiences with implementing five real-world scenarios for marketing and selling yourself as a professional speaker and trainer. Apply what is appropriate for you at this stage of your career and save the rest for later as you develop your practice and speaking business. Most likely, you'll eventually be involved with two or more of the following five key marketing strategies that are sure to help you build a profitable speaking and training career over time:

1. Back-of-the-room sales for your products
2. Royalties from books, DVDs, CDs, e-learning, and distance learning programs
3. Virtual store for product sales
4. Coaching and consulting appointments
5. Sample materials that promote your products

These are not the only ways to enhance your earnings, but in my experience, these strategies will boost your earnings and affect people way beyond the platform or podium.

Back-of-the-Room Sales

This is where you sell your products and display your marketing materials—in the back of the room. I always arrive a few hours early to set everything up. I travel with my own signs and I arrange my books and other materials in an eye-catching way for people who are walking by my display table.

I recommend going to a 24/7 place like FedEx Kinko's to get signs or banners made for your table. You can even produce merchandise such as mugs, calendars, buttons, and other graphics or giveaways. There are many companies on the web that can help you with logo merchandise.

It's All in the Presentation

Just like you want to look your best when you are on stage, you also want your product to look its best. It's all in the presentation.

At my presentations, my signs are prominently displayed with photos of the covers of the books I am selling and any bonus prices I might be offering for that particular group. I call them "bonus buys." Everything is colorful and easy to read. I always make sure the tables are covered with nice clean tablecloths, too. Whatever personal flair you can add will draw attention. I also display my full-color, two-sided postcards that promote each of my books. I use them as giveaways so people have a free bookmark or marketing piece from me personally.

Every speaker and trainer has their own special inventory of products they like to sell, depending on the venue. These can be books, DVDs, CDs, videos, manuals, and merchandise such as pens, mugs, and t-shirts. Whatever you are marketing and selling, keep it looking neat, desirable, and fun to browse.

Back-of-the-room sales also fall under the category of product sales at a convention or conference, where you have your own table or booth in the exhibition hall where you set up your items and sell them. I have done this as well, and it's a great way to meet conference attendees before and after a presentation.

I have done a variety of product sales over the years, and it is a lot of work, especially if you are on your own without an assistant. I always recommend getting help when you can afford to. Often the conference producers or meeting planners will have volunteers or assistants whom they are willing to assign or dedicate to helping you with product sales for a specific amount of time. Even if you don't think you will need help, take it. You will. You may have to use the restroom, take an important call, or speak to someone one-on-one. You don't want to ignore people who are holding up credit cards trying to get your attention.

Benefits of Hiring Help

If you don't have help, it can cost you a lot of money. I speak from experience.

At one of my keynote addresses, the client was happy to have me stay and sell and sign my books that I had on display at the back of the ballroom. There were 500 people in my session. The idea was for me to close my speech and turn it over to the emcee. I would then unhook myself from the cordless lavaliere microphone and get to the back of the room where all of my books and materials were displayed so that I could start selling and signing. But that's not what happened.

Before I could unhook my microphone, get off the stage, and start my way to the back of the ballroom, the 500 attendees, all freshly pumped up and motivated from my presentation, had already started to mob my table. My assistant was not there at that precise moment, and I was busy trying to swim upstream from the front of the ballroom to my own display table. I simply could not get through the enthusiastic, very loud, and ambitious crowd I'd just motivated moments earlier to jump out of their seats and run for my book display! It was a mob scene, pure and simple, and not being situated at my table, or having someone there ready to handle the enormous volume of people, cost me a bundle.

When people get to your table with wallet in hand, they do not want to wait even two minutes to buy your products. They want it right now, or they will get distracted and frustrated and walk to another booth or table and forget all about you. I lost quite a bit of earnings in sales that day, but the experience also has made me quite a bit of money over the years. How? I learned my lesson. I now always have someone at my table ready to take orders or sell products, even if it can't be me. My assistant or author escort and I switch off going to the restroom or getting a bite to eat. (I always bring my food back to the signing table, unless I am the luncheon speaker.)

So where do you find help? Ask the meeting planner or client if they have someone who can help you out for an hour or so. If you are a published author, meaning a publishing house represents you and you're not self-published, ask your publisher if they have author escorts in the area whom you can hire. Otherwise, find and train a person who will represent you well, is trustworthy with money, and can efficiently keep the line of buyers moving so that you can meet and greet attendees and sign books.

Make It Easy for People to Buy Your Products

If you have your signage made professionally and exhibit clear, easy-to-read pricing and special bonus pricing for conferences, you'll be off to a good start. I often use clear Plexiglas frames for my promotional signs so that I can easily slip out the old pricing and slip in the new pricing and any updates. I buy these at places like Target and keep a few extras on hand. I usually get the 8×10 size frames; they are easy to stack and pack for the road.

Accepting Credit Cards

If you're going to sell products, you've got to be able to accept credit cards, both online and in person. Lots of speakers and trainers use PayPal to accept credit card purchases; I think it is easy to use and a very good service. PayPal is a reliable source for setting up merchant accounts and accepts Discover, Master Card, American Express, and Visa. They also offer virtual terminals where you can receive payment by phone, fax, or email, as well as tips on how to increase your sales, and even shipping and tracking information on product sales. For other forms of credit card acceptance, check with your bank about rules and regulations for becoming a merchant and obtaining the equipment necessary to swipe credit cards.

Leave the Cash Box, Take the Calculator

Don't buy a cash box. Do buy a calculator. I say not to buy a cash box because it clearly tells the world, "Hey, there's a bunch of cash in here!" I use another kind of container that looks like it is used for something completely different from money. There are rare cases of theft at speaker events and in exhibition halls, but it does happen. I've seen speakers have cash or merchandise stolen, even their laptops. So pay attention. When there are hundreds of people around, it is easy to misplace an item or forget you've left something of value out in the open. Do buy a calculator, as that will make figuring up multiple sales and calculating taxes much easier.

Right before I am going to be doing a back-of-the-room sales event, I am sure to get lots of change, usually a stack of one-, five-, and ten-dollar bills. I especially have cash for making change when I am speaking in Las Vegas. Everyone pays cash in that city, and they expect you to be able to make change from hundred-dollar bills on the spot.

Use the Hotel's Safety-Deposit Box or Room Safe

No exceptions here. When you are carrying cash or credit card information, never neglect to use the hotel's safety-deposit box, or at the very least, the safe in your hotel room, usually located in the closet.

Royalties from Books, DVDs, CDs, E-Learning, and Distance Learning Programs

Did you know that while you were sleeping last night, you could have been cashing in?

One of the bonuses to having product lines and marketing materials as a speaker and trainer is that you can literally make money while you sleep. For me it comes in the form of royalty checks I receive quarterly or semiannually from my publishers.

While I am sleeping, someone in Bangladesh or Duluth is buying one of my books, DVDs, or CDs online or in a bookstore, and that translates into royalties for me that I collect on a regular and ongoing basis. I also earn passive income from royalties I collect from the e-learning and distance learning programs I have designed and developed for other organizations.

Books

If you write a book and a publisher contracts with you to publish it, then you will have passive income for some time, because the big publishing houses have the long arm of worldwide distribution that self-publishing does not always readily offer. (More on getting published for greater speaking opportunities later in this book.)

The Long Arm of Distribution Can Be Priceless. Once I turn in my book to my publisher and it is published, their distribution system takes over, and sales and marketing teams all over the world are selling my book to bookstores and corporations, as well as government entities. As a one-woman show, I would be hard pressed to reach that many people and get my books into major retail outlets.

An established publisher makes sure that your work is distributed worldwide. As an international speaker who works with multinational firms, this global reach is important to me. Therefore, I have always contracted with well-known publishers like ASTD Press and McGraw-Hill for my books. This is not to say that I don't think there is lots of great opportunity in self-publishing. You bet there is. But you must be prepared for what that choice will require of you as an author and distributor of your own books. I will cover publishing and self-publishing later in this book.

Making Money When Published by a Major Publisher. There are basically three ways that authors, like myself, make money on our books that have been published by major publishing houses. This does not pertain to self-publishing; again, more on this later.

1. We are paid advances and receive royalties on book sales (this includes all electronic books sales, such as e-books, and international sales rights).

2. We buy our own books from our publishers at a discounted rate and then resell them at events.

3. We reprint our own books when they go out of print under a contractual term called *reversion of rights* and then we can resell that book as a self-published entity, for which we now own the rights. Authors who self-publish usually do so with what is called print-on-demand. That means they print only the number of books they need at one time, which saves money and does not require warehousing of inventory. Smart! This way an author can order 100 of his or her books, have them shipped to the event where they are speaking and have them ready to sell at a profit. Profit margins on self-published books, however, vary widely.

People love to buy a speaker's books. And they really appreciate it when the books are signed. I've had many clients purchase very large orders through my publisher and then offer them to every employee as value-added giveaways at one of my corporate events. I always stay after my presentation to meet and greet the audience and to sign their books. Some clients even set up cocktail hours or meet-the-author receptions where the audience can mingle one-on-one.

Audio/Video, CDs, DVDs, and Custom Packaging

Many professional speakers and trainers make additional income selling their various product lines that include items such as audio/video, CDs, and DVDs, and the custom packaging they come in. Just as in traditional book publishing, there are commercial audio/video, CD, and DVD publishers out there, such as Nightingale-

Conant. Visit their website at www.Nightingale.com and consider the enormous possibilities for developing your own product lines. Check out Dr. Nick Hall's program *I Know What to Do, So Why Don't I Do It?* The professional design and packaging and credentials offered by Dr. Hall are the level of standard you want to strive to reach in this industry. When you visit Nightingale-Conant's website, click on Contact Us and get an update on the acceptance and status of product development ideas. Just as with a major publisher, they are overwhelmed with new product ideas and proposals, so acceptance of your product line may be difficult for a beginner. The next step would be to produce and package your own line of products independently. Most professional speakers and trainers do it this way with a great deal of success.

Producers and Packaging. First you must write your programs and books, and script your videos, CDs, and DVDs. Sound like a lot of work? It is. All of this develops over time. You can't rush it. I have written 12 books, but I did not write them all overnight. When I started out, I only had one book to sell. I also had one or two keynote speeches and training programs; now I have dozens of those, too, along with webinars, coaching sessions, and public seminars.

If you have the budget—the costs vary greatly depending on how many products you have and how sophisticated you want them to be—I would investigate putting together your own product line. I have worked with Janita Cooper and her team at Master Duplicating Corporation and recommend them to any professional speaker and trainer looking to create their own product line to sell at seminars or online.

Master Duplicating Corporation has an impressive client list. This company is turnkey and not only offers full video and audio production, but also in-house green-screen technology. That's the process of filming you in front of an all-green backdrop and then later dropping in a location or specific scene, such as somewhere you'd like to be—let's say at the site of an active volcano—or something you might be referring to in your presentation—perhaps the volcano erupting.

If you're interested in creating, promoting, and selling your own products, check out Master Duplicating Corporation's packaging and services on their website at www.masterdup.com.

Another well-known replication company that specializes in creating visually dynamic products, design templates, packaging concepts, and fulfillment is FlowMotion, Inc. You can sign up for their free newsletter subscription at their website, www.flow motioninc.com.

E-Learning Royalties

After writing my first few books, I signed a contract with one of America's top e-learning companies, MindLeaders, and was asked to contribute and author materials for a variety of e-learning video programs. MindLeaders is a premiere e-learning organization with more than 25 years of experience in the technology-based, self-paced training field. Their sophisticated and state-of-the-art e-learning tools cover topics ranging from leadership and management to IT solutions, and from healthcare privacy issues to a wide variety of business skills.

My initial involvement required that I write nine e-learning program script outlines. Each was produced by a professional team and turned into e-learning online video training. We even won a Telly Award (excellence in video production) for one of our programs. Writing e-learning programs for a company such as this, and there are many out there, is like writing books for publishers. Each continues to spin off royalties and exposure in a diverse and growing marketplace that I might never have had the opportunity to enter without my particular subject matter experience—the same expertise I use in my professional speaking and training career.

Distance Learning Royalties and Work for Hire

The popularity among professional adults in acquiring higher-education degrees via distance learning is exploding worldwide. Here's another venue for getting paid additional royalties on your work you may not have considered until now.

A few years back, I was contacted by a variety of universities both in the United States and abroad. Many had seen my book *Leaders—Start to Finish: A Road Map for Developing and Training Leaders at All Levels*, published by ASTD Press, and they wanted me to design and develop curricula for both undergraduate and graduate learning modules for their distance-learning programs offered online. I did and it paid off.

Some of my programs were work for hire, which means I was paid one flat sum for the entire program to which I sold the rights and license to use. For other curricula I designed, I continue to collect royalties from various universities or the academic IT service organizations that specialize in university online degree program engineering and development. These entities actually brokered my programs for the universities they represent worldwide. Presently, several of my undergraduate and graduate leadership programs are being taught online at universities around the globe. As I continue my involvement in this field, I design and develop updated curricula for a diverse and growing area of subjects. This exposure to a wide variety of academic communities has increased my book sales; several have now been adopted as textbooks or recommended reading by online professors for different management and leadership coursework.

If you'd asked me 10 years ago if my writing and speaking would evolve to this specialty area and spin off ongoing income years later, I never would have thought it possible. Being open to the possibilities in the world of professional speaking and training is the first step through the door of diversification of product lines for all of us in this business.

Virtual Store for Product Sales . . . .

E-commerce has become a very complex and often an expensive way to set up virtual stores, conduct product sales, and implement shopping cart features on websites. These websites are great when designed and implemented correctly (look at Amazon.com; they do a great job). Virtual shopping and features like shopping carts, however, also can become a monster of confusion and expense when done incorrectly.

Find a Reputable E-Commerce Company

Do your homework. Interview companies who have done this for lots of other clients like you. Get references and call them. Setting up a virtual online store with shopping cart features is a powerful marketing tool, but also it can be a powerful pain in the neck if it is not done correctly and set up by a respected company with a track record of specific experience in e-commerce solutions.

Unless you have more than one or two products to sell on your website, you may need only a payment page and not a shopping cart feature at all. I suggest starting small and let your site evolve over time. Do not fear. Your customer's needs will be revealed over time. Will international transactions be taking place? Will your customers need to access invoices at any time? Will there be recurring billing? What about returns? Will you need a tax calculator? What about security? How about real-time shipping?

Be sure to get what you want and ensure that you will have the flexibility you require as your needs change and your career evolves as a speaker and trainer. There's really no way to predict where your speaking and training practice will go. The possibilities are endless—e-commerce is changing, improving, and reinventing itself even as I write this.

My advice is to start small with a company where you call the shots and remain in control using customized solutions as you need them. Google terms such as *customer shopping cart, online shopping cart solutions,* and *e-commerce* to find companies and consultants that may match your needs and with whom you can have further dialog about expenses (it can be in the thousands), and what it's going to take to bring a positive virtual shopping experience for your customers and clients to your website.

Coaching and Consulting Appointments . . . .

Because I offer life coaching, I always have my life-coaching fliers with me at events. They sit on my book-signing table as a take-away. I've had many individuals come up to me after a speech and ask if I offer one-on-one coaching services. I then hand them my coaching flier (see Figure 5.1). With this information they can go to my website and click on the navigation bar where it says Arrange for Your Personal Life Coaching Session with Anne; this will take them to my page on coaching and my fees. Maybe my flier will help spark additional ideas for promoting your consulting or coaching services, if you offer them. I have spoken with several of my colleagues who use the opportunity while doing back-of-the-room sales to display their fliers on other services or products they offer. It's all about the spin-offs.

Sample Materials That Promote Your Products . . . .

Anne's Two-Pronged Approach to Using Marketing Materials

There are two specific marketing tools, besides business cards, that I use at almost every presentation I give—one-sheets and full-color postcards. They are very affordable and very effective in spinning off new business and referrals. It's not that they are so amazing or expensive or fancy. They are not. They do, however, leave long-lasting impressions on people and are fun take-aways that showcase what I can do for someone's organization.

I have been at conferences where there are speakers with all kinds of gadgetry and expensive giveaways. My observation is this: Most folks will stop and look, and take the speaker's give-aways, but they do not necessarily stop and talk with that person or read their information on the spot and ask pertinent questions that lead to almost immediate bookings. And that's where I seem to have hit the mark.

Getting to Know You

I make all of my handouts easy to read and easy to ask questions about. I recommend you do the same. I can't count how many people have read my one-sheet, for example, then asked me what my fees would be to come to their offices and do a workshop, or if I could speak with their boss the following week to discuss a possible speaking engagement at their upcoming manager's retreat in Lake Tahoe, or Las Vegas, or even on the coast of Spain. All of these instances panned out for me and I wound up doing the engagements. And they all came from simple, inexpensive but compelling marketing materials that had enough sizzle to get someone's attention and their eventual business.

One-Sheets

One-sheets are just that—one sheet, one side. Some speakers and trainers use both sides, but I still think one side packs more punch and looks more professional. A one-sheet sells you and your topics

FIGURE 5.1. ANNE'S LIFE-COACHING FLIER

on which you would like to obtain bookings. Some people call them content one-sheets.

What a one-sheet includes:

- a showcase of what you are selling—keynotes, training, seminars, books
- large header at the top of the page (mine reads: Bring These Dynamic and Entertaining Keynotes and Workshops to Your Organization)
- large footer at the bottom of the page with your contact info (mine reads: Visit www.annebruce.com for Free Tips, Tools, Techniques and More! Call 214-507-8242 for More Information & Scheduling)
- points you cover in your presentations and titles with bullet points
- endorsements
- mini-bio
- photo of you, caricature, or illustration
- easy-to-read large type with lots of color
- illustrations or photographs of your book covers or product packaging.

You can view lots of speaker's one-sheets online at their websites. You will typically find these under the heading One-Sheets or in the meeting planner or speaker bureau section of a speaker's website. Figure 5.2 is a sample of mine. After looking at how different many of the one-sheets can appear, start planning the layout for your own one-sheet. Again, my designer creates my one-sheet and I can always count on her to keep it looking current and fresh. Hire a designer to help you get your first one-sheet together and then be sure to update its content regularly.

FIGURE 5.2. ANNE'S ONE-SHEET

Affordable, Must-Have Marketing Materials

I will make this section of the chapter really easy for you with just one word: VistaPrint.

There was a time when printed marketing materials cost a fortune to produce, and the idea of doing anything in a full-color format was cost prohibitive for many people. The good news is that there are now many companies that can custom design and print your marketing materials. I prefer the simplicity and super customer service that VistaPrint provides.

I have been using them for all of my marketing materials for years, and they are truly a one-stop, turnkey operation for any business. Visit their website at www.VistaPrint.com for more information.

In addition, a service like this one can write and design your marketing materials in a few business days, including your logo, photos, or other images you want to incorporate into the design. They also offer a full gallery of more than 70,000 images. Prices are available online and will more than likely lower your current printing costs considerably. It did for me.

The Power of the Postcard Creates a Mini-Billboard

I mentioned earlier that I use full-color postcards to market my business at almost every event. I have found these to be extraordinarily powerful tools, especially when I am doing back-of-the-room sales.

For each book I am selling at an event, I display the books and my signage, pricing, etc. In front of each display I have stacks of the full-color, two-sided postcard that goes with each book. On the front, I have the book's cover prominently showcased and to the right of the book cover a photo of the author—that's me! Did you know that people are five times more likely to buy your product or service if there is a photograph of the person associated with that product or service? Photos breed familiarity, and that creates a comfortable selling atmosphere.

On the back, I include information on how to get the book and the bookstores that carry it, price, a listing of all my other published books, a plug for my radio show and coaching services, and, in bold print, my contact information—website, email, and phone. On some cards I do an oversize version (about 8.5" × 5.5"). I did this for my book *Leaders—Start to Finish* (see Figures 5.3 and 5.4); on others I have used the standard postcard size (about 5.5" × 4.5"; see Figures 5.5 and 5.6).

Creative Ways to Use Your Postcards

With rare exception, everyone wants to take postcards with them. I also find them to be great for customer receipts. If someone buys a book, I use the matching card as a receipt for that purchase and simply write on the back the purchase amount, date, conference attended; then I sign the card. This is much snazzier than using a receipt booklet from the local office supply store. Plus, that person then takes with them a way to find you again, or to look you up on the Internet, go to your website, or call you with an offer to speak at their company's next conference. These postcards also make very nice bookmarks for the book that is purchased. They are larger than a standard bookmark, so a person can jot down notes as they are reading, and they are pretty sturdy, too. The other use for these is that they are set up as actual postcards to be stamped and mailed to a colleague or friend, or used as a gift card inside the book that was bought for a friend.

Full-color postcards are much more than just free samples. They are mini-billboards that you can customize and with which you can generate leads and more business! They also can be used as impressive direct mail pieces.

FIGURE 5.3. ANNE'S OVERSIZED POSTCARD, FRONT

FIGURE 5.4. ANNE'S OVERSIZED POSTCARD, BACK

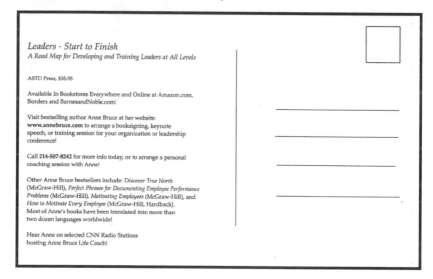

FIGURE 5.5. ANNE'S STANDARD POSTCARD, FRONT

FIGURE 5.6. ANNE'S STANDARD POSTCARD, BACK

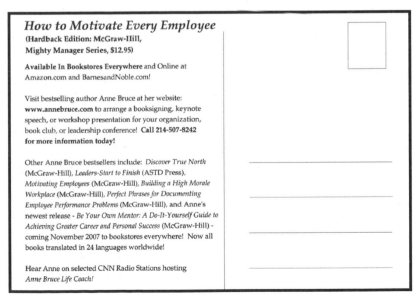

Marketing Materials That Make Your Business Sizzle

There are lots of other marketing materials you'll want to consider creating for your business:

- colorful and creative stationery kits and business identity systems
- full-color business cards with your photo
- customized speaker kit and press kit folders
- customized sticky notes
- creative mailing labels
- snazzy direct mail pieces
- full-color brochures
- inspirational or motivational card sets
- speaker showcase event invitations
- fun promotional items: t-shirts with your logo or slogan, pens, buttons, magnets, calendars, mugs
- Your own signature holiday, birthday, and special occasion greeting cards.

I hope these tips, tools, and techniques have helped you to generate your own creative ideas and flair for marketing yourself as a professional speaker and trainer. Once you're on your way to getting your marketing materials in order, you'll be ready to get moving on a strategic public relations and publicity campaign.

Keep It Legal . . . .

Unless you have the word *esquire* or the initials JD or CPA after your name, you will require the guidance of a lawyer, and a tax or financial advisor. I won't go into all of the various laws that can apply to copyrighting and selling products, but remember, as I've said all along, this is a business. The development of your product lines will require the advice of an intellectual property attorney.

Signed contracts and book deals usually require the guidance of a business lawyer; keeping records, selling merchandise, and paying taxes require the help of a bookkeeper, tax advisor, or CPA.

Do your homework up front and get advice from those who know the law. Tax laws vary from state to state and can be complex. There may be times you are required to collect taxes and other times you are not. Some states have reciprocity agreements, some don't. The main thing is to find out what your responsibilities and liabilities are when it comes to legal and financial matters regarding your speaking and training business. You're not running a bake sale for your son's soccer team. It's your career. It's your business. Treat it like one.

MAKING IT HAPPEN

- Understand the various types of products to develop so you can increase your revenue.
- Know how and when to appropriately market your materials.
- Get legal and financial advice when preparing, marketing, and selling your products.

 **Chapter 6**

Make Public Relations and Publicity Savvy Work for You

There are plenty of PR firms and services out there that specialize in representing speakers, and they can easily handle getting you publicity and media exposure. But what good are all those opportunities they unearth for you if you don't become a memorable and credible media resource to reporters? If you blow your first television or radio interview, you'll pay the price for a long time afterward. Print interviews are not any easier. Reporters remember who was a helpful and knowledgeable source on a story and who wasn't. They know who to go to and upon whom they can rely for accurate, up-to-date expertise on a subject and who gave them the best sound bites or quotes.

In this chapter, it is my goal to save you time, and I hope some money, by directing you to those I believe are among the best and most affordable resources out there for speakers, trainers, and authors.

Are You Media Savvy? . . . .

Know that the first step to developing great PR and publicity starts with you. Anyone can get some press some of the time, but the key is in becoming a savvy media expert and "go to" media source— someone who gives interviews on a regular basis because you are an authority. You may want to start by getting some media coaching so that you'll be ready when the opportunity presents itself.

Be a Newsmaker with Strong Sound Bites

A sound bite is a media term for a statement that the media will likely use because it is hard-hitting, is succinct, and clearly sums up your message. When you are watching the evening news and someone is being interviewed and he or she may have one statement that is aired, that's their sound bite. A sound bite is just that—a bite of sound from a lengthier interview—the statement that everyone wants to hear that sets you apart from the rest of the interviewees. It's memorable. For example, let's say a reporter is interviewing you about your book or speech on how you survived an airplane crash. You could say, "I knew we were going down; I threw open the emergency door on impact and started yelling for people to get out of my exit before the flames reached us!"

After my self-help book *Discover True North* was released, I was quoted in an interview as saying that "self-esteem is a person's intelligence in action." That sound bite was printed and run again and again. It caught editors' and reporters' attention because it implied that a person's self-confidence and self-esteem were an off shoot of their intelligence. That was not what it meant at all, but I knew it would grab the reporters' attention and was controversial enough to get the calls I wanted; then I could further explain what the statement was really all about on a variety of TV and radio shows and in magazine and newspaper articles. The sound bite simply meant that we all make smarter choices in life when we feel good about who we are inside. It had nothing to do with a person's IQ, as some assumed. The interviews brought a lot of attention to my book and boosted sales.

In another interview for a business magazine on employee performance, I said: "It's a myth that employees work better

The Press Release Read Around the World

Here is the press release I used upon the release of my self-help book, *Discover True North: A 4-Week Approach to Ignite Your Passion and Activate Your Potential.* Doing a run-of-the-mill press release on another self-help book would not have gotten much attention, so I focused on the controversy of saying that a person's self-esteem is directly related to his or her intelligence, which I write about at length in the book.

That statement got radio show producers and TV talk show producers buzzing, and magazines and newspapers calling me for interviews. It also resulted in two radio show programs I continue to host, called *Anne Bruce Life Coach.* The spin-off from this one release paid off in a hurry. But it was the structure and controversial approach that got people talking about my book and about me as a speaker. I was booked to do a keynote speech at a conference in New York two days after this release hit the newswires; I was paid $10,000 for that speech, plus first-class travel accommodations, which more than covered what I spent sending this release out over the wire services with PR Newswire.

This is the actual release and format in which it was distributed nationwide.

Your Self-Esteem Is Directly Related to Your Intelligence, Author Claims

NEW YORK, April 22, 2006 /PRNewswire via COM-TEX/—Self-esteem is directly related to intelligence and is actually your intelligence in action. That's the no-nonsense message from author Anne Bruce, who stresses the kind of intelligence she is talking about has nothing to do with a person's intellect.

"There are many types of intelligence—emotional, social, spiritual, intrapersonal, bodily, musical, and yes, even moral," says Bruce, whose latest book is *Discover True North* (McGraw-Hill, 2004). Bruce, who has written several best-selling books on human behavior and performance, says that if you have low self-worth, chances are good that one or more of your intelligences are also low.

"No one on this Earth can talk you into feeling good about yourself," says Bruce. "That is a choice that only we can make about ourselves."

The way Bruce sees it, every choice people make requires them to activate their minds and therefore their intellect, to tap into a wide variety of unique intelligences—like what Bruce calls **Choice Intelligence**, or **CQ (choice quotient)**.

In *Discover True North*, Bruce argues choices are not accidental discoveries. Rather, they are the brain in action, consciously making decisions that are a direct reflection of self-esteem.

"Each of us is the product of our own choice-making intelligence," Bruce says. "You will always attract to you the things you 'choose' to feel worthy of whether that be people, opportunity, or health."

Bruce deems the CQ the most powerful connector of our intelligence to our self-worth, good health, and ultimate happiness, and that the lack of it can easily sabotage intellect and ultimately self-esteem. That clears the path for depression, anxiety and other debilitating disorders that keep people from discovering their greater purpose, competencies, and talents, which Bruce labels a person's True North.

"If you use the American gross domestic product as a primary measure of prosperity in this country—although it has actually doubled in the last three decades—the proportion of our population that describes itself as sad, depressed and anxious has skyrocketed," notes Bruce. "What we think about ourselves is encoded into every cell of our body. We must understand we can never separate our brain from our body."

For interviews, please contact Anne Bruce by calling 214-507-8242, or by email at anne@annebruce.com. For Anne Bruce's biography, and more on *Discover True North*, click on http://www.annebruce.com/truenorth2004.htm, to download Word document graphics. http://www.annebruce.com.

under pressure. In fact, statistics show that when there's pressure, employees make more mistakes and have fewer new ideas." Or, one time for a major newspaper article on employee retention, I was quoted as saying, "The average cost to replace an employee can range between $40,000 and $100,000, or more!" I wound up on network television for that one.

Great sound bites are all about saying something right the first time, and then being able to back it up with facts and a credible, energetic interview. And that takes practice and media coaching. I've been fortunate. Years ago I was a producer for

CBS and I also had my own morning talk show for several years. I learned the business from the inside out, but not many people have this opportunity. Get help. Get professional coaching.

Get a Media Coach

Earlier in this book Lorri Allen, the Soundbite Coach, provided some great tips for emerging speakers. Lorri is one of the best media coaches, among other things, because she knows that what you're telling the world could greatly affect your bottom line—negatively or positively. Media coaches are in the business of helping people craft their message so that they can communicate with greater credibility and confidence.

For lots of free tips and tools on how you can become more media savvy, visit Lorri's website at www.SoundBiteCoach.com and subscribe to her free newsletter, *Media Savvy: eTips from the Soundbite Coach*, for media and PR tips.

What Media Coaching Can Do for You

Media coaching can be done in person or by telephone, or through email consulting. Check out a variety of people in the business and see what advantages and benefits they can offer you on your journey to speaking for a living and getting the press you desire.

Professional coaching can help you

- create a media policy for giving interviews and responding to crisis situations
- sharpen your presentation skills
- have more confidence in front of audiences
- polish your on-stage and on-camera presence and develop your radio presence
- formulate powerful sound bites

Ten Ways to Look Stupid on TV

It's easy to come across as an idiot on the television news. Believe me, even in these media-savvy days, people still freeze or become arrogant or develop funny accents.

To increase your chances of appearing on one of those funny video programs, should you ever be interviewed, please follow these steps to look stupid on television.

1. Say "uh," "er," or "you know" after every word. The reporter may tell you that the editor can remove excess verbiage. But the truth is, reporters are on deadlines and won't have time to make any edits.

2. Rapidly change your focus from the reporter to the camera. You may think you are establishing eye contact with both the photographer and the reporter, but you will look confused and shifty-eyed.

3. Use lots of foul language. Most broadcast stations will have to beep out your words and listeners will be so focused on what is being covered up, they will not hear the words between the beeps.

4. Ramble on and on, not making complete sentences. The editors will try to create a "sound bite," or a verbal quote out of your dialogue, but sometimes it's impossible and you can come across as someone who doesn't know when to shut up.

5. Pick your nose when you think the camera is turned away. The camera always seems to know when you're doing something embarrassing and chooses that exact moment to zero in on you.

6. Use big words and pronounce them incorrectly. I knew the executive wasn't that well educated when he proclaimed he was his own worst "critique" rather than "critic."

7. Attack the cameraman. These professionals are the ones that can show you in focus, or make you green. They like to be acknowledged and appreciated.

8. Lie. Your interview will be recorded and it may come back to haunt you. You may recall one world leader who was impeached, partly because he said on videotape that he "did not have sexual relations with that woman."

9. Wear plaids. Any pattern like hounds-tooth checks or plaids can cause the cameras to do what's called "phase" or "moiré." Viewers will be wincing so hard at your outfit, they will not hear your message.

10. Say "no comment." This makes you look evasive, guilty, and haughty.

You may find yourself being interviewed by reporters often, but these tips will also help you look stupid on video-conferencing, home videos, and even in presentations before audiences. Good luck—it takes little preparation and little creativity to be your best at looking stupid.

Source: Copyright 2007, Lorri Allen. Printed with permission.

- give you the critiquing you need to get better
- provide an analysis of your clothes, hair, accessories, and overall style
- prepare you for print interviews
- prepare you for electronic media interviews
- rise to the level of network television and radio interviews
- get professional on-camera training practice
- review your media kit, press releases, media statements, and all PR materials
- develop your long-term strategies for ongoing positive PR and publicity

- establish timely email consultations on a variety of media situations with which you may be faced
- look and sound your best.

I have always found that getting coaching in any area of your life where you might need some fine-tuning is a worthwhile investment. I say investment, because in my experience, there is always a significant payoff for having invested in oneself, especially when you're being paid to speak for a living.

Coaching Cuts Your Learning Curve

There's no doubt about it. There's a definite learning curve in this business. And if you are a novice, you may want to consider hiring a speaker consulting firm to start you off on the right track. And if you're a pro, then you know we all can use fine-tuning when it comes to sharpening our presentation and performance skills. The best in the business continue to get coaching and professional critiquing on their newest programs, while always looking to improve on-stage presence and style.

My best experience for this type of consulting and one-on-one coaching has been with Garrett Speakers International (GSI) and their speaker consulting division. All coaching is conducted under the guidance of Betty Garrett, who has observed many a novice who has fumbled trying to get an agent or bureau to represent them, or someone who tried to make it on the speaking circuit only to make costly media mistakes along the way. GSI has a division that does just that while teaming up with the best-of-the-best coaches in the business.

Speaker Consulting Survival Toolkit

I often refer to speaker consulting and coaching as a survival toolkit for new speakers. Here are some of the tools and coaching services you can expect when you hire a consultant to help you get into this business faster and more smoothly.

- initial consultation to determine your specific needs and learning opportunities as a beginning speaker or trainer
- up to six months of ongoing consulting
- scheduled conference calls as often as twice monthly and up to 60 minutes per call
- critical information and bureau-quality feedback through consultation, conference calls, and review of your speaker materials, which can include print, web, audio, video, and DVD packages
- names of selected vendors to launch your career, including but not limited to speech coaches, website designers, writers, printers, photographers, videographers, and more
- coaching on how speaker bureaus and speaker management companies operate and how you can work with them
- list of bureaus to contact once marketing materials are established
- review of your correspondence piece before sending information to bureaus
- whatever it takes to cut the learning curve shorter and get into the speaking business faster.

Speaker coaches and consultants usually charge a retainer fee; extraneous costs include the development of your materials, videos, and so on. For more information on Garrett Speakers International go to www.garrettspeakers.com.

Pitching the Media on Your Own . . . .

Unless you have extensive PR experience or take a lot of time to learn the game of pitching stories to the media on your own, there are some shortcuts you can take that will get your message out to the right media outlets and in the right format, greatly increasing the chances of your becoming a heavily quoted source.

My personal favorite and an organization I've held membership in for many years is PR Newswire, a world leader in the electronic delivery of information. Check out their website at www.PRNewswire.com, or call for more information at 888-776-0942. You also can email them at information@ prnewswire.com.

VNRs and ANRs and SMTs, Oh My!

I have placed many press releases and feature stories in the qualified hands of PR Newswire. Organizations like this one, and there are many, can help you to target your audience and reach influential reporters and producers domestically and internationally, at trade shows and conventions, and in local and national newspapers; as well as editors at specialized industry magazines, radio producers, network television producers, and more. They can tell your story to the world using audio and video webcasting and broadcast PR, such as video news releases (VNRs), audio news releases (ANRs), and satellite media tours (SMTs). An SMT is when you simultaneously see an author of a book on both *Good Morning America* and the *Today Show*. That author most likely gave an interview in a generic studio and that interview was then broadcast out to media in several locations, often on the same day. PR Newswire also offers electronic photo distribution.

More than ever, subject matter experts are being challenged to find new ways to get the media's attention. Hiring a service that can distribute your message to more than a half-million media points of distribution, plus help you to craft your message with expert editors and feature writers on staff, can be priceless.

Wire Services Cost Less than Postage

A standard news release that is sent over the wire will cost you less than postage. A standard release runs about 400 words. If sent to all media in your state plus trade publications, and then distributed to thousands of websites, online services, and databases, prices can run less than $200. If your audience is national in scope, you can target more than 22,000 media points for less than $700. If you've ever done any direct mailings, you know that these costs are much less than traditional mailing costs.

PR Newswire also offers its members helpful webinars on placing feature stories and more that you can sign up for. (Webinars are just like seminars, only they are conducted over the web, where audience members can participate in the discussion either out loud or by typing in a question.)

I recommend that you start first by writing your own press release and then handing it over to a major distributor like PR Newswire. And if your budget doesn't allow paying someone to do this for you, you can buy media lists online at affordable prices and send your press releases and features stories out yourself a little at a time. Just be aware that this is an extremely time-consuming project, and what would take a media distributor a moment to distribute worldwide, could take you weeks, or even months, of emailing and faxing.

Media directories and media lists also are available on websites such as www.mediacontactspro.com, www.easymedialists.com, and www.BurrellesLuce.com. Costs for partial lists can start at less than $199 and go much higher. Individual lists usually average about $200 to $400. The key is to work with list companies that keep their media contacts current and updated. A media list serves no purpose if the email addresses, phone numbers, or producers' and assignment editors' names are wrong.

These services offer more than just lists; they often include virtual media kits, complete with your own logo and links, free distribution with some companies, and updated media directories. They also offer features that include targeted media contacts, access to pertinent media contact data, help in locating publicity opportunities, and search features for editorial calendars, awards listings, and speaking opportunities.

Companies that sell their lists can make the entire process seem overwhelming; it can be if you are not clear on who or what media you want to target. Lists sold include weekly and daily newspaper contacts; radio station contacts; magazine contacts; trade publication contacts; ethnic press, such as Hispanic TV; all cable contacts; network news programs; news wire services; and more. With a simple click, you can buy any or all of these lists.

How to Be the "Go-To" Contact for Reporters . . . .

Finally, there's an even easier way to get your name in print, and it doesn't cost a fortune. I recommend using a proven resource called PR Leads.

This is not a book on do-it-yourself PR and publicity. If you're getting paid to speak, then you probably have newsworthy information that will get reporters calling you, instead of you pitching to them. PR Leads helps experts like you get the publicity you need to build your credibility to sell books, products, and your speaking and training services. A service like this one can be the fastest and easiest way, by far, to get publicity.

Dan Janal is the creator of PR Leads. Go to his website www. PRLeads.com and you'll find what I consider an amazing public relations and publicity service (see Figure 6.1). A big reason for this is that Dan knows the professional speaking business first-hand, because he's also a speaker, author, and area expert.

Seven Easy Pieces of a Press Release

1. FOR IMMEDIATE RELEASE—placed in the top left corner and all letters are capitalized.
2. Headline—This should be a grabber that tells the editor what this release is all about.
3. Dateline—City release is issued from and the date the release is going out.
4. Introductory Paragraph—This tells the reader who, what, when, where, and why. This paragraph must have a hook that gets the reader immediately involved.
5. Body and Content—This is where your message unfolds, or you can use an inverted pyramid approach and put the most important information first.
6. Your Standard Boilerplate—A short summation about you and your expertise.
7. How to Contact You for an Interview—Name, phone, email, website, and any downloads with graphs or illustrations, sidebars, or photos.

PR Leads won't accept a client unless they are confident that they can get you media leads and opportunities for interviews that are relevant to you. This service is not available to PR firms, large companies, nonprofit organizations, or educational institutions. PR Leads works only with authors, experts, speakers, and solo entrepreneurs.

If your budget allows, PR Leads can be a great investment for someone who's media savvy and ready to deliver compelling interviews. For about $100 a month, you'll get unlimited media leads in your major areas of expertise. PR Leads will send you relevant leads, but doesn't burden you with leads that waste your time.

FIGURE 6.1. PR LEADS WEBSITE

Source: www.PRLeads.com. Printed with permission.

How It Works

Once you've signed up for PR Leads, you'll be interviewed about your area of expertise and passion. Topics of expertise might include relationships, women's issues, business, sales and marketing, finance, home improvement, decorating, and so on.

PR Leads gets approximately 100 requests a day from reporters who are writing stories for major publications who need to find experts to quote in their stories. PR Leads sends you those reporters' names, email addresses, and story angles so that you can contact them directly. If you provide a good interview with the information that is needed, those reporters will write about or feature you in their publications. It's that simple. And we're talking big names like *The Wall Street Journal, Newsweek, The New York Times, The Washington Post, Redbook, Glamour,* CNN, and more.

When PR Leads sees a lead that matches your profile and expertise, they will send it to you by email. You will get a 100- to 200-word description of the article and its focus, the kind of expert the reporter is seeking, as well as the reporter's name, contact information, and deadline. You'll see the reporters' original request for an interview, unedited.

Make a Bold Impression with Every Reporter . . . .

This part of the book has been dedicated to helping you build your speaking and training practice, sell more products, get more speaking engagements and training opportunities, and make more money. But all of that starts by first building your credibility and then branding yourself as a subject matter expert.

People in general, the media included, want to know that they can go to someone who is different from the rest, an original, not a copycat. You've got to make a bold impression as a professional speaker and trainer if you are going to create a memorable brand for yourself.

Six Ways to Grab a Reporter's Attention

If you're new at this, Dan offers six ways to grab a reporter's attention and cement yourself as a future source and interview in media stories:
1. Focus on the news.
2. Give them unique information.
3. Provide facts, comments, opinions, or techniques.
4. Don't be pushy.
5. Don't self-promote. Just tell them what you do and how you want to be identified in the story.
6. Offer yourself as a resource for future stories.

What's Your Brand? . . . .

Brands are not just for products like the Coca Colas and Nikes of the world; they apply to people, too—especially speakers and trainers. Your brand is far more than just what you do. It is your signature style. It is what sets you apart from the pack. Author Tom Peters calls it *Brand You!*

The most successful paid speakers I know create their unique style, build a brand on it, and then boldly express themselves through that branding. In the end, that's what will make you memorable, not just to the media, but to your customers, clients, speaker bureaus, meeting planners, and the world.

MAKING IT HAPPEN

- Develop your media savvy and become a "go-to" speaker.
- Know what to expect from your media coach to help you look better and be more successful.
- Pitch the media successfully on your own by knowing the tools, lingo, and expectations.

PART THREE

Travel the World *Free* as a Speaker and Trainer

 **Chapter 7**

From Bozeman to Budapest: Speaking Can Be Your Ticket to the World

If you were to ask me to name one of the greatest benefits and perks I receive from being a professional speaker and trainer, it is that this profession has given me the opportunity to travel the world for free.

Many times I've traveled solo, and many times my husband, David, has accompanied me. I once spoke in Marbella, Spain, and my client provided my husband and me with a tri-level condo that overlooked the Mediterranean. Talk about a great environment in which to work! And recently my daughter Autumn met me outside of Albuquerque, New Mexico. After my keynote address, we had a relaxing mother/daughter weekend at a fabulous spa. My speaking and training events have taken me to four- and five-star resorts and locations worldwide. The people I've met and continue to correspond with have been the highlight of every trip. I have friends all over the world because of this career.

It's a given that as a professional speaker and trainer you will be traveling around the United States, but if you are open to international travel, the opportunity is there. In our post–9/11 world, I know there are speakers and trainers who are hesitant to travel internationally, but I have found it to be the great expander of my career and my life.

Your Book, Bureau, and Internet World Tour

Later in the book I discuss how book publishing and using speaker bureaus will help you travel the world. But in this chapter, I focus on speaking internationally. Having books published and being represented by speaker bureaus is a big help if you want to travel. I have found, however, that the Internet and my website have created a sort of international meeting spot for anyone interested in bringing my programs to their country.

I do a lot of international speaking and training; I would say that 90 percent of those engagements come from my website and my books, which have been translated into more than 24 languages. When a potential client in Europe, let's say, buys my book, they will contact me about presenting one of my seminars based on it. For me, this is where many of my spin-offs are born.

Bridging the Culture Gap

If you want to speak internationally, you need to create a page devoted to international speaking on your website, provided you have some international work experience. My website, www .AnneBruce.com (click on the International Speaking link) highlights my experiences in addressing international audiences at worldwide conferences and seminars (see Figure 7.1). For example,

FIGURE 7.1 ANNE'S WEBSITE

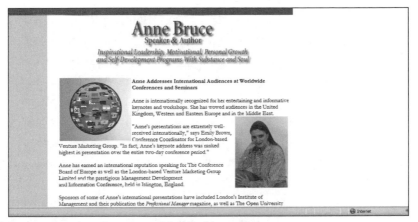

Source: www.AnneBruce.com. Printed with permission.

I am proud of having been a speaker for the Conference Board of Europe, its HR Council, the Polish Marketing Council, and the Polish Human Resources Council of Warsaw. I've also done extensive work in the Middle East, an area of the world many female speakers have not yet tried, and so this experience sets me apart. I continue to do a great deal of work in the UK and so I highlight that experience and my work with MDI (Management Development and Information Conference) and the Institute of Management in London.

My international speaking page on my website also mentions my engagements in France, Geneva, Italy, the Netherlands, and Spain. The purpose is to have representatives of multinational firms who are visiting my website see that I have worked in both Western and Eastern European countries extensively, as well as the Middle East, and that I am comfortable doing business with a wide and varied group of cultures. I also include a list of U.S.-based world-class and internationally based companies I've addressed, including Sony, Johnson & Johnson, Ericsson, Arthur Andersen, and Nestle.

Pack Your Passport

It may seem ridiculous to mention this, but I will anyway. Do you have a passport? Fewer than 4 percent of U.S. citizens hold passports; a much smaller fraction ever use them. If you don't have a passport, get one; if it's expired, renew it. As a professional speaker and trainer, you can't afford to miss out on any international speaking opportunities. Suppose you got a call to speak in Paris and you didn't have a passport or it had expired? You would miss a great life experience that would expand your international speaking portfolio.

Also some international locations will require that you have a visa, so check with whoever is booking your travel on whether or not you need a visa.

Are You Experienced?

Don't take on international speaking assignments for the money. Do it for the experience. I'm not saying that you should not be paid, but it's important to realize that international organizations often do not pay the going rate that you might command in the United States.

Some speakers and trainers mark up their domestic rates to cover travel time and the inconvenience of being out of the country. But unless you're a celebrity, that method will usually price you out of the international market.

If you normally get $5,000 for a workshop, you may have to take $3,500 in a foreign country. Always quote the client your fees in U.S. dollars, not the currency of the country in which you are going to be working. Try to make up the difference in your fees by negotiating extra days at the event's hotel, sightseeing tours, or upgrades to business class seating on your flights.

Companions Pay Their Own Way

Whatever you do, *do not* expect the client to pay for your companion's airfare, meals, attendance at an event, or any other extraneous expenses. The hotel room you will be staying in is about all you can expect to be covered when you take someone with you. I have always set up a separate expense account for my husband when he travels with me so that none of his charges appear on the clients' portfolio. Everything is kept separate and my clients always appreciate that.

And even though the pay may not be as high as what you would get paid in the United States to speak, you may indeed get multiple bookings, and so the sheer volume of your work and the experience of visiting a foreign country makes it all worthwhile. I was once offered a six-week European assignment by a client; my husband, David, and I turned it into a wonderful working holiday and he simply paid his own expenses.

When it comes to money and international speaking, the dilemma is often to go or not to go. But don't base your decision strictly on fees when a romantic dinner atop the Eiffel Tower can turn an everyday workshop into a lifelong, memorable experience.

Turning Euros into Dollars

Some speakers are leery of doing international events because they fear they may not get paid, or that the group is legitimate. First, before accepting the offer, which you will ask for in writing, ask the client for names of other speakers in the United States you can call for a reference. Call those speakers and ask about timely payment. I have done this with every international client I have worked for and no one has balked.

Next, require that the client direct book your airline tickets and hotel accommodations, and request a 25 percent deposit to hold the date. Require that you be paid in full, including per diems, via wire transfer of monies to your account in the United States, on the day of your arrival. Some speakers request this one week before they arrive. Ask that the client provide you with a receipt of deposited funds into your account. Don't insult the client by asking for "proof."

I've been working internationally for many years as a paid speaker and trainer and I've never been "stiffed," as some call it, or mistreated by an international client. In fact, the only times I experienced issues with client payment have been when I was booked to speak in the United States—and usually for prestigious, large firms. But again, this is an exception, rather than the rule.

Parlez-Vous Francais, Y'all

You're not in Kansas anymore, Dorothy. If you intend to speak at an international event, approach your assignment with consideration and politeness, respecting all cultural differences.

Whenever I overhear an international client saying something negative about a U.S. speaker, it is usually that the speaker was insensitive to their culture, or that the speaker came across as arrogant and disrespectful. There is absolutely no reason for this to happen. Often it's our American characteristics of being a bit too outgoing, overly friendly, and informal that can send a much different message on foreign turf.

Remember these three things and you'll be ready to speak globally:

1. **You are an ambassador first and foremost.** One of the wonderful opportunities about working in the international workplace is that we get to be ambassadors for the United

States. Opinions of Americans may be formed by western movies and television sitcoms, but mostly those opinions are formed by you and how you respect and treat others when speaking in a foreign country. Don't forget the golden rule—treat others as you would be treated—whether you're in Denver or Dubai.

2. **When in Rome** . . . well, you know the rest. Impatience overseas will get you nowhere fast. For example, when dining in Spain, you are expected to take your time and enjoy the meal. Tapping your foot for the check because you have scarfed down your dinner and are ready to leave is not in keeping with the culture in that country, where dining is a slow and deliberate affair. Relax.

3. **Pack a positive attitude along with that passport.** When you're working abroad, you'll need a positive attitude and sense of humor. Things are different in other countries. Instead of acting the bemused observer of other people's idiosyncrasies, raise your glass and cheer, "Vive la difference!"

Anne's Cross-Cultural Business Etiquette Tips . . . .

We live in a global society. Whether the presentation you are making is in Philadelphia or Singapore, you will most likely have delegates from many cultures and nationalities in your audience. A diversified understanding of various cultures, because you've experienced them firsthand, will endear you greatly to your audience and international clients and speaker bureaus.

Here are some tips I teach in one of my seminars on doing business overseas.

- **Prepare yourself for the culture you are going to be working in.** Taking time to study the cultural habits of a foreign country will help set you up for greater speaking success once you get there. I recommend travel guides like the Lonely Planet (www.lonelyplanet.com) and DK Publishing's Eyewitness Travel Guides (www.DK.com). There's simply no excuse

An Interview with a Successful International Trainer and Speaker

I first met Robi Bendorf when we were both on the same speaking platform at a series of seminars in London. A few months later, I saw Robi again in London. We realized that we were both to be speaking at the same time that October in the United Arab Emirates, where we decided to hook up and share ideas on international training. Robi, who'd been there many times before, showed me some of the sights of that extraordinary area.

I believe the reason that Robi is such a popular speaker, whether he's in Pittsburgh or Rome, is his respect for all cultures. Robi's niche is consulting and training, including purchasing and global sourcing, supply management, export development, and international contracting; his clients include Westinghouse Electric Corporation, Duquesne University, Johnson and Johnson Medical, Corning, The Walt Disney Company, Chevron Texaco, and SAE International. He can be reached on his website, www.bendorf.com, or at info@bendorf.com.

ANNE: What are the hurdles you face as a trainer and speaker facilitating programs from one country to another—Dubai one day, Paris the next? What are the greatest advantages to you as a speaker?

ROBI: Hurdles are the frustrations of air travel, getting food one is familiar with at a reasonable price, and the initial set-up in each venue with different hotel staff, languages, different power systems, different projectors, and room setups. The secret is of course to maintain your sense of humor, and of course, topping the list is to hope for a good pillow. The advantages are what you learn from attendees and meeting extremely interesting people.

ANNE: How do you stay so energetic working in so many international times zones then going home to Pittsburgh for family time?

ROBI: Time zone issues for me are fundamentally mental. I just act like I have always been in the new time zone—I never even think about it. One trick I use on myself is to change my watch to the new time zone as soon as the flight takes off.

ANNE: What has been your greatest enjoyment as a trainer all these years? What is it you take away from your audiences that makes you better each time?

ROBI: Training internationally is extremely humbling in that the attendees are usually having to deal and cope with extremely difficult situations, and even though the trainer may not have been in that specific situation, the real enjoyment comes when the trainer's experience and knowledge can lend assistance that is immediately recognized by the attendee. Training as a profession demands constant learning. The take-away is that as we learn more, the knowledge glass does not become fuller, instead the glass becomes larger, so that even though we learn more, the percentage of what we know compared to what we want to know is decreasing—providing us with a never-ending opportunity of discovery.

ANNE: What is your advice to those starting out when it comes to developing business and working in the international workplace?

> **ROBI:** Know very clearly what you want the business scope to be, understand clearly what part you will play in providing the scope, gain total understanding of the market, determine your niche in the market, and stay focused on that scope and niche. Many people start out with too many scopes. Unfortunately, spreading around your effort on too many scopes usually means that not enough work is performed on any one of the scopes, resulting in none being realized.

not to be somewhat knowledgeable about other cultures before you arrive.

- **Study international business etiquette.** Take time to learn the appropriate etiquette and different social mores of another nation, especially if you are going to be dining with clients in another country. For example, in some places in the Middle East, women do not dine with men. In the UK, everyone is very conscious of manners, so turn off that cell phone. Tipping and other rituals can vary greatly from country to country as well. All of this information is available in handy, easy-to-carry pocket guides, or can be quickly downloaded.

- **Be ready to work with interpreters and translating equipment.** Practice before your presentation if you are using translating equipment, just as you would any other equipment you'd be using in a presentation anywhere. Also take time to talk with translators who might be in the room and ask them how you can best accommodate them, the pace at which they'd like you to speak, and how much pause you should give between examples. Americans talk much faster than most, so slow down your pace and speak clearly.

- **Avoid slang.** Try not to use slang or informal phrases. For example, "Can you get that to me ASAP?" or "That fellow is really barking up the wrong tree." The group you are speaking to in Japan might not understand your colloquialisms.

- **Don't be arrogant when replying to questions from your audience.** At a conference I was speaking at in Germany, there was a presenter who went on before me. An audience member offered his own company's way of handling a project, and the speaker replied, "Well, that's not the way we do it in the United States." This statement gave the entire audience the impression that this man was showing off. And he was. Another audience member quickly quipped, "Well Mr. Brown, in case you didn't notice, we're in Munich, not in Cleveland." International speaking engagements require that a speaker be aware that what may be suitable or appropriate in one location, does not automatically make it appropriate for another. So ditch the "our way is the best way" superior attitude.

- **Always be aware of your body language.** Again, be aware of what's appropriate for where you are. For instance, sitting with your legs crossed in some countries is considered impolite, but it's acceptable in the United States. Know that direct eye contact, which establishes quick credibility in our country, is an invasion of privacy in many Asian nations. Instead, gaze across your audience and you won't embarrass anyone. And smile. That's a form of universal communication understood around the globe.

- **Follow protocol and observe customs and rituals.** Take time to research the business protocol of the country you are visiting and working in. In some cultures, jokes, casual attire, and other informal behaviors are not acceptable. For example, when speaking in the Middle East, conference producers ask that speakers build into their programs several required prayer breaks throughout the day.

- **Gender plays an important role in other countries.** Gender plays a key role in almost all foreign travel. In some countries where gender is rooted in the tenets of religion, mistakes can prove unforgivable. For instance, when I traveled in the Arab world, my clients could not shake hands with me because touching a woman other than your wife is forbidden there.

- **What to do when it's cocktail hour.** In Russia you're expected to drink to establish relationships. In France, wine is the alcohol of choice. In Australia, alcohol is discouraged at business functions.

- **The rules on gift giving vary.** The main rule on gift giving is that the gift be of quality. If your gift has your logo on it, be sure it is discreet. Do not give logo gifts in Greece, Portugal, or Spain. In China you should never open a gift in front of the person who gave it to you. But in Africa, gifts are opened immediately and with gusto!

- **Don't let jet lag affect your performance.** Get plenty of rest before your trip. Being sleep deprived makes jet lag worse. For long trips with many time zone changes, I always arrive a few days early so that I can adjust. I have discovered that jet lag is more a state of mind than anything else. With a few common sense practices, you can be ready to take the stage refreshed anywhere in the world.

Travel Will Make You a Better Speaker and Trainer . . . .

Wherever and however you live in your own city or state in America is not how the majority of the planet lives and works. Travel is a great wake-up call for a professional speaker. It makes us more sensitive to others—their life struggles and hardships, their political views, and cultural values. Trust me, there's more to the world than what is shown on the 6 o'clock news. How will you connect to our global workplace and the multinational organizations and their people that you hope to address and affect? Travel will connect you to your speaking audiences in ways you never imagined.

When I travel to do a speech, whether it's to Texas or Poland, I always experience a sense of exhilaration and excitement, and that fuels my presentation and greatly benefits my audience. When speakers explore the world through both domestic and international travel, they quickly step into other people's maps of the world and out of their own. When we do this we gain greater perspective on the world, greater compassion, and greater appreciation for one another's differences. Don't you think all of those things could make you a better, more powerful speaker and trainer? Can you just imagine the stories you will be able tell in your presentations?

I have eaten fried camel in the Middle East at a colleague's home. I've had coffee and conversation with men and women who escaped persecution and communism in Eastern Europe. I've taught classes to one-time poverty-stricken Nigerians, and I've spent time with heads of state and political figures, like former Secretary of State Dr. Henry Kissinger. All of these life experiences came to fruition because of one thing—I speak for a living.

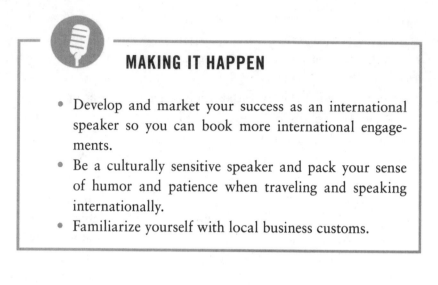

MAKING IT HAPPEN

- Develop and market your success as an international speaker so you can book more international engagements.
- Be a culturally sensitive speaker and pack your sense of humor and patience when traveling and speaking internationally.
- Familiarize yourself with local business customs.

 **Chapter 8**

How Important Is Being a Published Author?

IN THIS CHAPTER . . . .

- Publishing books will make you more in demand
- Pros and cons of traditional and self-publishing
- Do you need an agent?

To write a book or not to write a book—that is the question. It's a good one. Does getting published help you build a profitable speaking career? Yes! Getting published in one form or another becomes the foundation that will provide your speaking career with

- enhanced your credibility as a subject matter expert
- content for a media kit
- entry to more publications and editors
- access to other media, such as TV, radio, Internet exposure, and others.
- business leads for more engagements
- handouts
- the basis for eventually writing a book.

It's a Step-by-Step Climb to Getting Published . . . .

If you've never been published, it's a step-by-step climb, especially if you're headed to the big publishing houses in New York. Everyone wants to see what you've had published first before doling out publishing contracts.

Your publishing efforts may start out with something as simple as a newsletter article and then develop into an article for a community newspaper, leading to a piece in a local daily or regional newspaper, and then perhaps on to national magazine or trade publication. You also may land interviews, or find your tip sheet in a prestigious publication, such as *The Wall Street Journal* or *San Jose Mercury News*. After all of that, you may have a shot at getting published by a major publishing house.

I speak from experience when I recommend the step-by-step climb to getting published. I took all of these steps before I had my first manuscript published. This book you are reading now is my twelfth book by a major publishing house. But none of it happened overnight. It took me years and a systematic approach to get these books under my belt and options on others to come. Where are you now and where do you want to be?

Speaker/Authors Are in Great Demand . . . .

I can tell you, yes, there is definitely a trend toward greater success for speakers who have been published. Speakers who are authors are in much greater demand by bureaus and event planners than are speakers who don't publish.

Being a published author can increase your speaking and training fees significantly. It was not until my first book was released that I was actively pursued and represented by speaker bureaus and invited to address audiences outside my own backyard. When my first published book, *Motivating Employees*, hit bookstore shelves, it cranked up my value as a paid speaker and trainer tenfold. I instantly became a credible authority on the subject of motivating employees and building a high-morale workplace (which happens to be the title of the sequel to *Motivating Employees*).

You also will find that when your books are translated into foreign languages and sold worldwide, this automatically increases your offers to speak internationally. I soon discovered after writing *Motivating Employees*, followed by *Leaders—Start to Finish, Building a High Morale Workplace*, and then *Perfect Phrases for Documenting Employee Performance Problems*, that U.S. management books and seminars on these subjects were in high demand overseas. It seemed that everyone wanted to know about the tips, tools, and techniques that we are teaching here in the United States. Managers in other countries wanted to learn how they could modify and adapt to their own cultures the management techniques that were so popular here in the United States. My body of published work catapulted my speaking and training career like nothing else ever has. And the more books I write, the more work I get.

The Great Debate: Traditional or Self-Publishing . . . .

There exists a snobbish attitude when it comes to getting published: If someone doesn't pay you to publish your book, you're not an author. That simply is *not true*. If you require that your ego be stroked daily, then get a dog.

Paid speaking and training requires all the tools you can muster to be successful. How you go about getting those tools and then selling them to customers is up to you. The fact is your success will have little to do with who publishes your materials and more to do with how you promote and market yourself and your materials.

Here are the criteria I recommend in helping you decide which route of publishing is best suited to your individual needs—traditional publishing or self-publishing methods.

When Traditional Publishing Is Right for You

* You are seeking the highest international credibility available as an expert or authority in your field.
* You are an accomplished writer and want to build an association with a major publishing house.
* You are willing to take the time to write a book proposal and then pitch that proposal to all relevant publishers. (This is a very time-consuming effort.)
* You do not want to be bothered with having to handle all of the production, distribution, and marketing of your book.
* You would rather concentrate on getting more speaking and training bookings then becoming a book publisher and distributor.

When Self-Publishing Is Right for You

* You want to say you are a published author and you want a book published fast—90 days or less.
* You are not a writer and need to hire a book doctor or ghostwriter to help you complete a book.
* You need a product to sell at seminars.
* You want to take control of the entire publishing process for your materials and have a system in place to market and promote your books.
* You are not interested in mere royalties on a book; you want to keep all profits for yourself.

Once you've decided which method of publishing is right for

you, consider some behind-the-scenes tips on how to make it all happen and what to expect in the process.

Beating Down the Doors of the Big Houses . . . .

Traditional publishers are often referred to as the "big houses," as in publishing houses. A publishing offer with a major publishing house is hard to get. It's very competitive. Big houses get thousands of book proposals submitted to them every year. But so what? If you're confident of your material and your writing talent, then go for it. And once you're in, you will have an easier time getting attention on your next book. That still will not preclude you, however, from having to do a full-blown proposal, marketing research, and all the rest that's required.

Publishers Love Self-Promoters

Big publishing houses love professional speakers and trainers who promote their books at their speaking engagements. Every time I submit a book proposal to a publisher, I am asked to include a calendar of my speaking engagements for that year and beyond. Today's publishing houses want to contract with authors who want to be partners in actively marketing and selling their books. The days of the publisher turning over a finished book to the marketing or publicity department and then relying on those sales efforts alone are over. Today, authors get very involved in the marketing and promoting of books published by even the biggest publishing houses.

To have your book proposal accepted by a major publisher is very gratifying. Notice I said *proposal*? Do not write an entire book and submit it to a publisher. They hate that. Editors want to see a proposal and an outline with a full marketing plan first.

Here's a tip that will save you lots of time and frustration: Visit any publishing house's website, and you will find a link called *submissions*. This will tell you exactly what the publisher is looking for and even provide you with an outline of how to construct your book proposal. Simple, huh?

Follow the publisher's requests for submissions to the letter. I cannot tell you how many budding authors I've spoken with who do not follow these submission guidelines, but instead, submit what they think the publisher needs to publish. They will never land a big-name publishing house with that approach. You've got to give publishers specifically what they want and how they want it. Otherwise self-publish.

And forget putting into your book proposal that you have the only book ever written on this subject and that no one else has ever written anything like it. That's a deal killer. Publishers want to publish books with popular topics and that are in demand with audiences. No one is going to want to publish your one-of-a-kind topic. For example, there are a million relationship books out there. Why? Because almost everyone is interested in bettering their relationships, or repairing them, or finding them. The key to pitching a book like that is not having the only one out there, but having a unique spin that stands out from the pack—but you're still part of the pack. Even Dr. Phil is part of the pack, but he has his own unique Texas-style, in-your-face approach that's gotten him tons of play and even a TV show.

Publishers like proposals, outlines, marketing plans (tell them how you're going to sell this book), and chapter samples so that they can modify what you send them to meet their specific publishing needs. Remember, it's a business. Every large and small publisher wants to know how much money they can make on your book and how you can help them make it. Let the publishers run their business and you run yours. If you do, you'll make a great author/publisher team.

Writing Tools You Can't Live Without

- *The Writer's Market* (Writer's Digest Books)
- *Jeff Herman's' Guide to Book Publishers, Editors and Literary Agents* (Three Dog Press)
- *Guerrilla Marketing for Writers: 100 Weapons for Selling Your Work* (Writer's Digest Books)
- *Getting Your Book Published for Dummies* (Wiley Publishing)
- *How to Write a Book Proposal* (Writer's Digest Books)
- *The Complete Guide to Book Publicity* (Allsworth Press)
- *1001 Ways to Market Your Books* (Open Horizons)
- *Speak and Grow Rich* (Prentice Hall, Revised and Updated Edition)
- *The Complete Idiot's Guide to Getting Published* (Alpha)
- *The Right to Write* (Tarcher Putnam)
- *Stephen King on Writing* (Scribner)
- *The Elements of Style* (Allyn and Bacon)
- *How to Get Happily Published* (Collins)
- *Agents, Editors and You* (Writer's Digest Books)
- *Writer's Digest Magazine* (www.writersdigest.com. Buy a subscription; you'll be glad you did.)
- All of the Writer's Digest Books (the most helpful of all how-to writing books on the market).

Do You Need an Agent to Proceed? . . . .

To date, I have never had an agent. Now, if I were to write a novel, you bet I'd be beating it to New York to find a literary agent to represent me. However, for trade publishing in general, I have found that with a little research and legal counsel, you can do this on your own.

An agent will take a commission on your book sales and those commissions vary. On your own, you can expect royalties to run between 10 percent and 15 percent of the price of the book as a general rule. These numbers change depending on the amount of sales, international rights sold, and e-books and books on tape/CDs that are sold.

Advances are usually reserved for authors with at least one other book published, but not always. And unless you are Anne Rice or Stephen King, don't expect more than a $10,000 to $40,000 advance. There are, however, some high-profile professors who get $50,000, even $100,000, in advances on their books. These monies are then deducted from initial royalty checks. It's pay now or pay later when it comes to advances.

Pros and Cons of Traditional Publishing . . . .

Pros

- You will reach a worldwide market of buyers and readers who never would have known about you.
- You will get bookings from the tremendous reach of your publisher that you never would have gotten alone.
- There will be fewer hassles for you—no need to worry about production problems, layout, ISBNs, bar coding, cover design, editing, printing, warehousing, or fulfillment.

Cons

- It is difficult to get a major publisher to accept your manuscript and offer you a publishing contract.
- You have no control over the price of your book.
- You have no control over production of your book.
- You may not have a say in the title.

- You may not be happy with the finished product and parts of your manuscript that have been edited out.

Just like professional speaking and training, the business of becoming a published author with a major book deal is extremely competitive and requires lots of hard work. But if speaking for a living and getting published by a big publisher were easy, everyone would be doing it, right? And that's the attitude that will set you apart from the rest.

Self-Publishing: Hall of Shame to Hall of Fame . . . .

I would venture to say that self-publishing has become the rule rather than the exception in the speaking and training industry. What used to be considered the hall of shame or vanity publishing is now the hall of fame when it comes to famous books and authors who first self-published.

There have been many self-publishing success stories in recent years. Yes, it is now possible to self-publish and get the same respect as you would get from publishing with a mainstream publisher. Paul Nathan, former *Publisher Weekly* rights columnist, once said, "Gone are the days when self-publishing was virtually synonymous with self-defeating."

Many famous authors were rejected by traditional publishing houses and forced to self-publish. This didn't stop them from getting to the top of their profession. Did you know that bestselling books like the first *Chicken Soup for the Soul, The Bridges of Madison County, What Color is Your Parachute?* and the *Diary of Anne Frank* were all at first self-published and later picked up by major publishers? And famous authors, such as Deepak Chopra, Pearl S. Buck, Gertrude Stein, Edgar Allen Poe, T.S. Elliot, and Ernest Hemingway were all self-published authors until they found their niche and audience that would support their work. Even Dr. Seuss was rejected 24 times by publishers.

And now there's print-on-demand, which offers a great way to test the market for your book. With print-on-demand, you can literally print one or 1,000 books at a time. If you're a speaker who can really get out there and market your book, then there's even a chance that you could sell the reprint rights to a large publishing house.

There are lots of quality self-publishing services out there that you can Google and research, but one I like to recommend is iUniverse (www.iUniverse.com). They are a full-service, affordable, turnkey operation for someone who wants to go this route. They are affiliated with Barnes & Noble, but Barnes & Noble, like many booksellers, will usually not stock self-published materials. If you use a company like iUniverse to publish your book, it can be ordered directly by customers, libraries, or from bookstores through the iUniverse website. Your book would also be available through Barnes & Noble, but not on their bookshelves in brick-and-mortar store locations. You also could place orders at online retailers, like Amazon.com. With iUniverse, your book automatically is listed with *Books in Print,* and your contract is nonexclusive, meaning you control your own copyright. They will, however, control the pricing of the book and royalties paid to you simply because they are doing all of the work, instead of you publishing the book on your own with a group of independent contractors who transform your work piece by piece into a professional quality, print-ready manuscript.

One of the greatest advantages to working with iUniverse is that it is very fast. You can get your book published in just 30 to 90 days after you submit your manuscript in final form. In the traditional world of publishing that timeframe is much longer.

When you research the multitude of choices available to you in the world of self-publishing, you'll find that even though paying to be published is not always acceptable to everyone, it is preferable to many.

Here are some of the reasons why self-publishing might be your best choice to boost your speaking career as well as the drawbacks to consider.

Pros and Cons of Self-Publishing . . . .

Pros

- Your proposal or manuscript won't be turned down.
- You receive all the income from sales; however, with a full-service publisher like iUniverse, you are paid royalties.
- You control the formatting, production, cover art, and editing.
- You control all publishing rights.
- You eliminate all the barriers of traditional publishing and time restrictions.
- A book can be done by anyone with the financial resources and time to devote to the project.

Cons

- You don't get the credibility that a recognized publishing house offers.
- You take all the risks and do all the work.
- You will be hiring editors, designers, and a printer independently and then coordinating all of the production (unless you go with a turnkey organization, such as iUniverse and others).
- You will be handling ordering and fulfillment, as well as accounting.
- The entire process can be very expensive.

- Unless you are signed on with a major book distributor, self-published books are not stocked in bookstores, or in airports, like traditionally published books are.
- Book reviewers and newspapers will not review most self-published books.
- You will be completely responsible for your book's sales and distribution, and all of its marketing, promotion, and advertising.

Compilation Publishing

The other avenue some speakers and trainers take is to be part of a compendium or compilation of short stories within one bigger book. Some of these publishing opportunities, for which you pay a sizeable fee to be a part of, are actually considered more marketing tools than traditionally published books. Here's how it works.

The promoter markets a book and theme to a speaker desirous of getting published, usually through emails. For a fee, the speaker can have his or her own chapter in a book, along with big-name authors, such as Les Brown, Deepak Chopra, or Mark Victor Hansen. The pitch from these companies is that you will have a "back-of-the-room" product to sell at your next speech, and you will be able to make a profit from your sales.

The organization usually conducts a brief interview with you for your chapter's content and has you respond to some questions in alignment with the book's theme (faith, leadership, customer service, motivation, and so on) with your own quotes and replies. They will then send your chapter back to you to review. From there they do all of the formatting and design work, which turns out to be about 15 to 20 pages in length.

Each book has a custom front cover. The marketer places your photo on the cover along with the big-name authors I mentioned. When the product is completed, the marketer will then sell you the book. An example of how this is done may look like this: You are offered 1,200 books, let's say, for a total cost of $4,000. That makes each book's cost $3.33, before shipping and taxes. Then the recommendation is made that you resell your book at one of your seminars or training events for a profit. The marketers will often suggest a retail price, such as $19.95 and then remind you that you can net a hefty profit of $19,944 when you sell all these books. What they may not mention is that it will be very difficult to sell 1,200 books at any one time, at any event you do, and that you may be toting home boxes of books to store in your garage until the next event.

I'm not saying that this venue isn't right for a lot of people. In fact, I think that it can be a unique opportunity for the right speaker. But for most savvy audiences, the credibility of such a publication may be lacking. Do your homework. Investigate any and all organizations that market such creative publishing opportunities. Examine the pros and cons, and then make your best decision based on the way you operate your speaking and training practice and how you want to be perceived. In addition, some of these marketing companies will cross-sell their inventive publishing opportunities with promises to list you with their speaker booking agency, or market you to meeting planners. This may or may not be an effective or credible alternative.

Other publishers will give you ready opportunities to publish pamphlet-style books. These, too, are usually sold in limited volumes or online, but never in bookstores and never with the same credibility of a book designed in a traditional book format, even if it's self-published.

"I Can't Help Thinking There's a Book in This" . . . .

Before you enter the publishing world, know why it is you are publishing anything to begin with. What are your reasons for doing this, and what do you hope to accomplish in the end? Is it to

- impress family and friends?
- gain greater publishing recognition?
- fuel your speaking and training career?
- make money?
- help others?
- get booked on *Good Morning America*?
- confront and deal with personal issues that you want to resolve? Act as a catharsis?

Before you put your fingers to the keyboard, answer these questions and move forward in a direction that will ensure your ability to speak for a living.

MAKING IT HAPPEN

- Publishing books will make you an in-demand speaker.
- Know the differences, pros, and cons of traditional versus self-publishing, and decide which one is right for you.

 **Chapter 9**

Signing Up with a Speaker Bureau

People ask me all the time, "How did you get an agent?" "How did you get listed with several speaker bureaus?" Without a doubt, there seems to be an uncanny interest among emerging speakers and trainers in breaking into what is thought to be an elusive and exclusive speaker bureau club. But the fact is, that club really doesn't exist for most of us.

Speaker bureaus can provide excellent networks for speakers and can change the status of someone's career, but they are neither required for success nor are they something that works for every speaker and trainer. They are, however, considered the big pond for big fish in the industry.

I am represented by three speaker bureaus, but none of them is the size or magnitude of a Washington Speakers Bureau, for instance. My agents are not asking themselves, "Do I book Colin Powell for this engagement, or Anne Bruce?" Some of the bureaus I work with book me to do keynote presentations at events or to

How Does a Speaker Bureau Work?

Speaker bureaus are a great resource for organizations, meeting planners, and event coordinators. Large bureaus sometimes represent thousands of speakers. It is the bureau's job to bring their speakers' expertise to the attention of their clients and to find a good match for the client's event. A bureau's fees are paid out of the fees charged by the speaker, not by the clients they represent.

do training or breakout sessions at conferences. The frequency of my bookings from these bureaus varies and can be up and down, and that is to be expected. Over time you build relationships with owners of the bureaus and that continues to keep you "top of mind," but with others, it may be strictly business.

My experience with bureau owners and agents is very similar to those relationships I have with editors and publishers. They are the hardest-working people you will ever meet. I always appreciate the business bureaus give me, and I respect their decision to book another speaker if I am not the right fit.

Avoid My Mistakes

When I started out speaking and training for a living, I called the Harry Walker Agency in New York to see if they wanted to represent me. Yeah right! This is the agency that represents big names like Wolf Blitzer, Bono, and her Majesty Queen Noor. I didn't even have a book published at that time. It was foolish of me to have pursued them, not to mention that it was a waste of Harry's receptionist's time to even have taken my call. But my point is this. Harry Walker himself had the courtesy to call me back and encouraged me to keep moving forward in this business. I was truly a no-name in the field, and he was kind enough to give me advice and to point me in the right direction. I never forgot that. I have never been represented by this agency and most likely never will be. Their clients are the celebrity rock stars of the speaking circuit and as I said in chapter 3, I am a making-a-real-good-living-speaking speaker.

Find the Right Bureau Fit

Know your strengths. Align yourself with the bureaus with which you can work most effectively, bureaus whose clients and meeting planners you can benefit most and that can benefit you. Even if you were to get listed with a big bureau, you would still be one of hundreds of speakers listed in its database. There's no guarantee that you'd ever get a booking. Being associated with the most prestigious speaker bureaus is an ego trip for most speakers. Focus instead on creating and building relationships with the bureaus that are best suited to your category of speaking and the talents, subject matter, and competencies you have to offer. And be patient. When I first got accepted as a speaker with Eagles Talent Connection, Inc., out of New Jersey, I did not get booked to speak right away. But I kept my profile "top of mind" with the agency by building relationships and continually updating my speaker profile and video demo. I eventually made the short list for an event, but oftentimes I did not get chosen. However, that did not discourage me. Eventually, the perfect engagement presented itself and I got a call from Eagles Talent representative Bill Lee. Bill, a recognized pro in the business, worked with me and the client to ensure that I was the right fit for the right engagement. That solidified an ongoing relationship with a highly respected and high-profile speaker bureau. Being patient paid off for us both. I was ready to swim in the bigger pond and, therefore, didn't sink.

If you get listed with a bureau from a big pond and you're still a little fish, you'll just get eaten. Either the bureaus never call you, or when they do, they place holds on dates with you and then release them. That's no way to speak for a living.

How to Get Noticed . . . .

If you want speaker bureaus and event planners to notice you, then focus first on building your speaking and training business on your own. Create a website with sizzle and punch, and get out there and speak. All of the speaker bureaus I presently work with came to me because they'd heard about one of my presentations, saw me speak, read one of my books, or visited my website because someone referred them.

Let's say you get that long-awaited and wished-for call from an agent at a speaker bureau. They have a booking that you might be a good fit for. It's in Chicago for a major insurance company on May 8. Are you ready? Do you have a first-class speaker package or kit ready to send them via overnight delivery? Do you have a link on your website just for bureaus and event planners where they can download your bio, stream video, view your one sheet, read client testimonials, and more? Do you have a commissionable fee ready to quote?

Remember, bureaus will take 25 percent to 30 percent of your fee as their commission. If you have a problem paying this size commission to a representative, then don't. Get your own bookings and keep the entire fee. My feeling about paying these commissions is that I would never have had the business if not for the bureau, so I am more than happy to pay their much-deserved commission. The last thing is this: Do you charge at least $3,500—preferably $5,000—minimum for an engagement? The reason for this is that your fee has to be worthwhile to the bureau. If your fee was only $2,000 for a speech and the bureau got 25 percent, they'd only be getting $500 for the booking and that would be considered a waste of their time. If that same bureau books a speaker for $10,000 and gets 25 percent, then their commission would be $2,500 and much more worth their time and energy to pull you into it. As I said in the beginning of this book, speaking for a living is a business first.

What You'll Need to Swim with the Big Fish

- Develop first-class speaker kit, including professionally produced video of you "live" in front of an audience speaking or training—total cost for a complete speaker kit can range between $15,000 and $20,000 and up, depending on the quality of production of your materials.
- Charge fees starting at least at $3,500 to $5,000.
- Provide one-sheets.
- Include bio.
- Create postcards and promotional materials on books you've written or products you sell.
- Include your top three program titles and let the bureau know if you do breakout sessions, training workshops, book signings, panel discussions, consulting, coaching, or if you have products to sell.
- Name the industry you specialize in, such as pharmaceutical, law, technology, etc., and include that in your packet—don't just say associations and corporations.
- Name other speaker bureaus that have actually booked you in the past.
- Include references and testimonials from clients.
- Have a complete office setup for sending and receiving faxes; a dedicated business phone line; an account with FedEx, DHL, or UPS to get packages out even when you're on the road; and a fast, mobile way to get back to the bureau with your availability, within an hour or two max, from wherever you are once you're contacted—immediacy is key in this business.

Don't waste an agent's time if you are not ready to swim with the big fish in the big pond. If you're still in guppyville, then you're not ready to work with a bureau.

Most bureaus post their specific requirements for how to get listed with them or how to become one of their speakers on their websites. And just like the publishing houses who post submission requirements for book proposals, bureaus expect you to give them precisely what they require to make a decision on listing you with their firm. The closer you get to meeting their criteria, in both cases, the better the chances you'll land a big pond bureau or big house publisher.

Debunking the Myths about Speaker Bureaus

The more you know about speaker bureaus and how they function, the better the chances you will have of building a strong relationship with one and getting booked to give a speech. (Keep in mind that meeting planners and event planners are usually the customers of the speaker bureau and work through them to find speakers for annual meetings, special events, and training sessions.)

I have included Betty Garrett's article *Seven Myths about Speaker Bureaus* here because I strongly believe that it not only debunks the myths that meeting planners have about working with bureaus and agents but also will give you, the speaker, a good idea of how bureaus work behind the scenes and what's required to swim in their big pond.

Speaker Showcases and Contests

In this business there are a multitude of speaker showcases and contests that take place. Some of these showcases and contests are run by meeting planners and some by bureaus. The purpose is to showcase or spotlight up-and-coming speakers. For some of these

Seven Myths about Speaker Bureaus

Myth #1: Speaker bureaus only book celebrities and top billing personalities such as Colin Powell, Maya Angelou, Lou Holtz, Anthony Robbins, and Terry Bradshaw.

Fact: While those speakers are available, quality speaker bureaus work with ALL budgets. Not every event merits a high-end speaker; however, every event deserves a professional speaker with a proven performance record regardless of the size of your budget.

Myth #2: Speaker bureaus add more hassle to the meeting professional because they create a middleman.

Fact: Actually, speaker bureaus facilitate the process for meeting professionals because there is only ONE contact person to assist you, not the many representatives for each individual speaker. A quality bureau will eliminate your headaches, while streamlining the process and paperwork.

Myth #3: Speaker bureaus cost more to use.

Fact: Absolutely not! Professional speakers pay the bureaus out of the fees they would charge a client. It costs no more to use a bureau than to go directly to the speaker. For the same price structure, a bureau acts as a resource for you and your group.

Myth #4: Speaker bureaus are never around when you need them; they go home at the end of the day.

Fact: Unlike the professional speaker who is always on the road traveling from event to event, a bureau is stationary and can send materials at a moment's notice. A quality bureau will always give you an emergency number so you have 24-hour access to them.

Myth #5: Speaker bureaus only "sell" their speakers.

Fact: Almost all independent bureaus have a core group of speakers who produce consistent results and have earned the bureaus' respect. However, we constantly research and identify those speakers who are the best match for your group. Some speakers own their own "bureaus." Therefore, their agenda to promote a particular speaker can be influenced by their personal desire for the speaking engagement. The owners of GSI are *not* competing with our speakers; our advice in your selection process is unbiased. We have thousands of speakers we can research to fit YOUR particular need.

Myth #6: Speaker bureaus do not care about the outcome of your event.

Fact: A professional bureau has a vested interest in making sure your speakers are a success and that you receive the standing ovation you deserve. The owners of GSI have been on both sides of meeting planning. We understand that there is nothing more painful than being in the audience and realizing the speaker you have hired was not a fit or did not perform to your expectations. If the inevitable happens and a speaker cannot honor his or his commitment, a bureau can help you find a solution. Using a speaker bureau is like having good insurance…you need a back-up plan and support when the unexpected happens.

Myth #7: Speaker bureaus are interested only in a one-time sale.

Fact: Good speaker bureaus are interested in long-term relationships with their clients. Consequently, we become information resources for the meeting professional. We can be as involved with the decision-making process as needed. Many times clients look to us for topics, trends, and determining who and what is hot in the market. Your continued satisfaction is our utmost concern in our dealings.

events you must be selected to participate and for others there is an open-call where you can pay to be previewed by experts and bureau owners in the business.

A Word about Contracts . . . .

Contracts with bureaus are proprietary and, therefore, I cannot print one here. You can call and ask for a sample contract; many bureaus are happy to send them to potential speakers. Every bureau is different: Some have lengthy and complex contracts and others don't. Either way, they typically are templates that you will see again and again and will become accustomed to signing and understanding the fine print.

Some of the things you might expect to find in a speaker bureau contract might include, but will not be limited to

- agreed upon speaker fees to be paid to the speaker, when and how this will be done, and the commission rate to be paid to the bureau, and when and how that is paid
- method of payment, terms and conditions, such as the client shall pay 25 percent down to the bureau to secure date (also referred to as the holding deposit), and that the balance owed shall be paid directly by the client to the speaker the day of the presentation and that you agree to send a bill to the client for expenses within one week after your presentation, or that a per diem will be included in the total amount being paid to you.
- any restrictions placed on speakers regarding ongoing contact with the bureau's client
- your travel requirements and equipment requirements
- any business and inquiries, or spin-offs, from this client at any future date (sometimes there is a specified time, like two years) that shall be booked for you by the bureau

and that you will refer all contact and negotiations to the bureau

- contact between speaker and client, which is often not allowed and includes product sales, consulting, and training offers, unless contacts are first referred to the bureau who originated the booking—these rules vary greatly from bureau to bureau
- sometimes general speaker etiquette, which is covered in bureau contracts and may include points such as the speaker should not charge incidentals to a client's master account, or that a speaker agrees not to engage in vulgar language or use inappropriate, off-color materials, get drunk, or other unprofessional behaviors while working the booking, both on and off the platform.

Should You Pay to Be Showcased?

There are bureaus that charge to showcase talent, and in some instances, that can be a good way for a new speaker to get in front of bureau agents and their clients. Ask around and see what amount of business other speakers have gotten from being a part of these events. Whether or not to participate is your call. If you feel you have a shot at getting in front of important decision makers who might never have the opportunity to see you in action, then by all means, take your best shot if you can afford to do so.

If you are just starting out and are relatively unknown in the business and all of a sudden you are approached by a group or bureau that wants to charge you to be a part of their showcase—proceed with caution. These folks are often making more money on hopeful speakers' dreams than they are on booking them. My advice is to wait until a bureau books you at least one time before paying them money to showcase you, or at least talk to other speakers affiliated with the bureau to see what experiences they have had participating in such showcases.

Prestigious showcases you may want to be a part of include the annual International Association of Speakers Bureaus convention and the annual National Speakers Association convention. Check out their websites for details, and talk to some bureau owners who are members to see if they might be able to get you onto the showcase after viewing your demo video and speaker package.

One other warning: There are companies on the Internet that prey on hopeful speakers by claiming to have big marketing campaigns in which they will market you to thousands of meeting planners and others for a cost of $500 or more. They usually claim to have limited slots available for these campaigns in order to create urgency on your part. My recommendation: Save your money and invest it in building your speaking practice on your own. The idea of speaking and training for a living is that you are the one getting paid, not the other way around.

When You Make It Big

When you've really made it big and you're getting dozens of speaking engagements a year, you may want to consider the services of a speaker management company. One of the best is SpeakersOffice, Inc. Visit their website at www.speakersoffice.com. Other prestigious firms include the Speaker Management Company, at www.speakermangement.net, and CMI Speaker Management, at www.cimispeakers.com.

What's the difference between a speaker bureau and a speaker management company? The management company manages your travel, calendar, follow-ups to leads, etc. They are paid on a retainer basis, plus a commission on bookings. They are the business managers of the speaking world. The difference between the two organizations is that speaker bureaus do not have full control over speakers' calendars like management companies do. Bureaus also do not book a speaker's travel, hotel accommodations, etc.

(although the bureau's client often does), they do not get paid a retainer either, only a commission.

Typically, speaker management companies will handle only a small select group of world-class speakers, whereas a speaker bureau will represent many more. The significant difference between the two is that a speaker management company will provide a range of essential business and marketing services to a speaker, including bookings, and a bureau will focus mainly on handling your bookings.

More Resources

I have provided a Speaker Bureau Networking Toolkit online for you to download and use. It lists speaker bureau contacts and other helpful resources. (See Appendix A for a list of the toolkit contents as well as download information.) *Do not* submit an e-blast to all of the bureaus listed! That would be very unprofessional. Take your time to review each bureau and their websites. Investigate what they require to be listed with each of them.

- Ask yourself, "Does this bureau work within my fee range and in my genre?"
- Check out the bureau's reputation with both speakers and clients. Do their clients meet your criteria? In other words, why would you want to be listed with a bureau that only books jugglers from circus acts, when that's not what you do in your act?

This networking toolkit is simply a starting point to begin the process of matching the best bureaus and their clients to your best talents and competencies. Review chapter 2 where I emphasize finding your niche and keeping your focus. When you do, you'll be ready to step into the spotlight.

MAKING IT HAPPEN

- Know how a speaker bureau works and what it can do for your career.
- Find the right fit for you and your speaker bureau choice.

PART FOUR

Step into the Spotlight

 **Chapter 10**

Becoming *Almost* Famous: Defining Your Success

This last part of the book focuses on the final action step you must complete if you are to make it in this business—and that's stepping into the spotlight.

You've been reading about what it's going to take to speak and train for a living and get paid well for doing it. Now it's time to get out there, take the stage, and become what I like to call *almost famous*. Being almost famous is not the same thing as being a movie star or world leader. You know you've become almost famous in this business when you are known enough in your area of expertise that people recognize your name, remember reading your books, or come to see you speak again because they enjoyed you so much the last time they heard you. That's being almost famous.

Fight for Fame or Get Sucked into Anonymity . . . .

Speakers and trainers who are almost famous naturally draw more business and quality referrals to them. (Refer to the cycle of abundant speaking and training in chapter 1.) And although it seems like an effortless endeavor to outsiders, the truth is that even at this stage of your career, it's still a lot of work to maintain what you've built.

Once you've hit this milestone in your speaking career, it's not about being all things to all audiences. It's about having just a little fame among all the right people in your genre. It all comes down to targeting the right markets and developing a mini-celebrity status and solid reputation in your specific area. It means you've avoided what professional speakers and trainers dread most—anonymity.

Working in a global marketplace means that the number of speakers and trainers competing with you for the same clients and customers continues to grow exponentially. Clients and customers aren't looking in their own backyard for speakers and trainers; they're scouting the entire world via the Internet. You've got to fight for your little bit of fame and keep fighting to hold on to it, otherwise you can be sucked into the dreaded black hole of anonymity. How can you keep this from happening? Get creative, be original, brand yourself, and don't swim in a sea of look-a-likes. How will you differentiate yourself from the pack? What can you do to maintain visibility, enhance credibility, and establish a greater brand name reputation in your area of knowledge?

The best engagements will come from those who have heard about you, read about you, or seen you speak. Afterward they will want to meet you and ask you to sign their book, get your advice, and tell their friends about you. It is truly the most humbling and gratifying experience you will have as a speaker and trainer. To know that you have actually helped someone, moved them to action, or given them hope for a better tomorrow is the reason we all do this job for a living—to enhance the lives of our audiences.

This book has covered numerous ways for you to build your personal brand and skill set as a speaker and trainer. Now I'm going to share with you how I've used my almost famous status in the speaking and training world to step into the spotlight and produce my own series of public seminars.

Step into the Spotlight: Produce Your Own Seminars. . . . . .

Becoming a seminar producer is not for the faint-hearted. It's by far the highest-risk venture in the speaking industry. It also can, however, produce the highest profit of any speaking venue. Producing your own public seminars is definitely one way to step into the spotlight, as speaker and producer.

Public seminars are sold to the public and are open to anyone who wants to pay to attend. There are many speakers who produce their own seminars and market them to all kinds of audiences worldwide. You've probably heard of Tony Robbins and his famous seminars that he holds at his own private resort in Fiji. People pay thousands of dollars to attend his events.

A Good Day at the Office Defined

The specialized audiences who will attend public seminars are endless. I, too, launched my own series of public seminars about five years ago and I continue to offer them to this day. I don't charge thousands of dollars to attend, but I do charge $495 per person to attend my popular *Author's Life Retreat*. If only 25 people enroll, it's a good day at the office, even after expenses.

When I became a published author, I realized that wherever I went to speak or do a book signing, the number one question I'd get asked was, "How can I get published?" That was the seed that grew into my *Author's Life Seminars and Retreats*. I tested these seminars first by rolling them out at Barnes & Noble bookstores that carried my books. I did this for free to test the waters, and Barnes & Noble ran the publicity campaigns and printed up big posters with my picture and the cover of my book on them and then placed them in their store window displays. The response was overwhelming, and so I soon launched my own public seminars at four-star hotels in various cities. The flier on one of my public seminars (see Figure 10.1) was from the event I did in Charleston, South Carolina.

This flier was emailed to hundreds of people in the area. I also ran weekly newspaper ads and did a national features release through PR Newswire (see Figure 10.2). The release was printed in newspapers and on Internet news sites, such as CBS, KRON in San Francisco, and many more. I had an assistant to help me with the two-day event. We had aspiring authors from all over the United States attend my seminar and retreat.

It bears repeating, that producing and marketing your own seminars is a lot of hard work. You will have to make all the arrangements yourself, including writing press releases and features, pitching media, securing hotel meeting space and hotel rooms, arranging for meals, ordering equipment for the seminar, writing workbooks and copying materials, designing posters and e-letters to promote the event, faxing, producing fliers, taking care of refreshments on site, hiring someone to handle registration and back-of-the-room sales, and a million other small details necessary for pulling off a successful seminar.

Start Small and Grow Your Seminars over Time

I now produce a number of my own seminars and retreats, but I started out small. Did you know that many well-known speakers started out doing seminars in their own homes? The creator of Weight Watchers, Jean Nidich, for example, started this way.

FIGURE 10.1. *AUTHOR'S LIFE RETREAT* FLIER

March 5-6
Learn How to Become a Published Author

- Get Started as a Writer
- Get Published
- Sell Your Book
- Hotel Accommodations
- Fee

Get Started as a Writer

Anne Bruce

Bestselling Author of books such as *Be Your Own Mentor, Discover True North: A 4-Week Approach to Ignite Your Passion and Activate Your Potential, Leaders—Start to Finish, How to Motivate Every Employee, and Building a High Morale Workplace*

Get Published!

Charleston Place Hotel
205 Meeting Street
Charleston, SC 29401
March 5-6

Author's Life Retreat
Presented and facilitated by bestselling author Anne Bruce

Greetings! "If you want to be a published author, here's where to start. I hope you will join us for this one-of-a-kind seminar and retreat."

Sincerely,
Anne Bruce

If you've always wanted to write a book, but weren't quite sure how to get started, what to write, or how to find a publisher, you'll want to attend this practical, no-nonsense workshop with Anne Bruce, bestselling author of books such as *Be Your Own Mentor, Discover True North: A 4-Week Approach to Ignite Your Passion and Activate Your Potential, Leaders—Start to Finish, How to Motivate Every Employee,* and *Building a High Morale Workplace.*

Register Now!

Day 1
The Good, the Bad, and the Ugly of Getting Published—Behind the Scenes Tips and Tools of Writing Books for a Living
- Jumpstart Your Writing Life—From Inspiration to the Written Word
- Author/Publisher Relationships
- How You Will, or Won't, Make Money as an Author
- Publishing Contracts, Self-Publishing, On-demand Publishing, and Literary Agents
- Importance of Editor Etiquette
- Beware of Publishing Scams!
- Author's Toolkit—A Great Takeaway of Handouts for Ongoing Reference and Help

Day 2
Marketing Yourself as an Author—Book Tours, Book Signings and the Media
- Stepping Into the Spotlight
- How Successful Authors Sell What They Write
- Packaging and Promoting Yourself as an Author
- Turning Your Book Into A Keynote Speech, Seminar, Workshop, or College Course
- Author's Toolkit—More Handouts and Takeaways for Marketing Yourself as an Author

FIGURE 10.2. FEATURES NEWS RELEASE

FEATURES EDITOR

IF THAT PUBLISHER'S JUST NOT THAT INTO YOU, FIND OUT 4 KEY REASONS WHY AT *AUTHOR'S LIFE RETREAT* IN CHARLESTON

CHARLESTON, SC, February 3, 2005—*Author's Life,* a two-day seminar & retreat, will be presented in Charleston, SC, at the Charleston Place Hotel, on March 5 & 6, by bestselling McGraw-Hill author and life coach Anne Bruce (*Discover True North: A 4-Week Approach to Ignite Your Passion and Activate Your Potential, Motivating Employees, Building a High Morale Workplace, Leaders—Start to Finish,* and more).

"If you've always wanted to get a book published, but instead, you have a drawer full of rejection letters, this would suggest—that publisher's just not that into you!" says Bruce, "and here are some reasons why."

- You didn't research the publisher and then follow the submission guidelines.
- You thought you could write well enough to get published.
- You expected a publisher to "fix" your manuscript.
- You jumped the gun by writing the book first, instead of the required book proposal.

All of these things and more can set up an aspiring author for rejection. Bruce's program focuses on what publishers really want from authors, how much money authors can expect to make, and how to avoid publishing scams that take an author's money only to leave them with a box of books and no book distributor. Bruce says that after taking her seminar, writers will know exactly how to go about getting a *legitimate* publishing contract. Some of Bruce's tips to authors include:

- **Be able to demonstrate to a publisher a plan to market and sell your book.**
- **Give publishers what they ask for by following specific submission guidelines.**
- **Focus on writing a great book proposal first, not an entire book.**
- **Legitimate publishing houses do not ask you to pay them!**

According to Bruce: "Eight out of ten people say they want to get a book published. It doesn't matter if it's a children's book, novel, science fiction, business, or self-help book—the key is knowing exactly what a publisher is looking for, being able to meet deadlines, and fully recognizing the discipline and focus required to actually complete a book from start to finish. This is the ideal program for anyone who's serious about becoming a published author."

For information, or to register, visit: http://www.annebruce.com/authorslife.htm, or call 214-507-8242, or email Anne at anne@annebruce.com. Website: http:www.annebruce.com.

I still like to do seminars in small settings and in my home or other people's homes, especially when I am facilitating weekly workshops on my self-improvement book *Discover True North*. I call them *Discover True North Expedition Groups*, and they are held in groups of 15 or fewer participants, in a small, intimate setting.

Here's a thought: You also might want to consider getting a co-producer to help you with your first run at this.

Landing Sponsorships for Your Seminars . . . .

Getting paid sponsorships for seminars and workshops or to sponsor just one keynote presentation has become quite popular. I have had newspapers and magazines sponsor me. I've also had associations, and even cruise lines, pay my fees in exchange for the promotion they received that was related to my event. When you land a sponsor you have a written agreement. The sponsor gets promoted via your speech, or seminar presentation, and your speaking fees and expenses are paid by the sponsor. I'm sure you can imagine the combination of opportunities that exist here.

Lots of specialty seminars, like those for physicians and dentists, for example, are sponsored by organizations, like pharmaceutical companies. Professional seminars often charge attendees several thousand dollars per person and offer continuing education credits.

Affiliate Your Speaking and Training with Continuing Education Accreditation. . . . .

A note about accreditation: If you affiliate your seminars and programs with professional accreditation, it can greatly increase your seminar's attendance. Many of the university programs and private seminars that I have facilitated have been approved and recognized by the world's top accreditation bodies, such as CPE (Continuing Professional Education), ILM (Instituted of Leadership and Management), REP (Registered Education Provider), and the ICC (International Code Council). Investigate the possibility of getting your seminars and workshops accredited with these prestigious accreditation bodies. You'll be glad you did, and you'll be almost famous when it's over.

MAKING IT HAPPEN

- Build and maintain your success by drawing more business through quality referrals.
- Find and keep the spotlight by successfully marketing yourself and producing your own seminars.
- Increase your seminar's attendance by affiliating your seminars and programs with professional accreditation.

 **Chapter 11**

The Journey to Speaking: From There to Here

Everyone follows a path in life that is just a little different from the one the guy next to them is traveling; speakers are no different. We come from all walks of life, all different points of origin, too. On your own personal yellow brick road to becoming a professional speaker or trainer, you must have come from somewhere, be it chasing tornados in Kansas or teaching tourists how to surf in Waikiki. I've asked several speaker friends to share where they came from and what worked for them in becoming and staying successful in this business. Becoming a polished and savvy speaker is a labor of love, one I'm sure you'll enjoy as you journey out into finding your own Oz.

NSA and the Certified Speaking Professional Designation . . .

The first step on your path should be toward the National Speakers Association. NSA was founded in 1973 and provides resources and education to advance value of not only its members but the entire profession as well. I recommend that hopeful speakers check it out at www.nsaspeaker.org. Annual subscriptions to NSA's popular *Speaker* magazine are also available online at its website, www .nsaspeaker.org, and you do not have to be a member to subscribe.

The Certified Speaking Professional (CSP) designation is the speaking profession's international measure of professional platform skills. The CSP designation is earned through demonstrating competence in a combination of standards:

- professional platform skills
- professional business management
- professional education
- professional association.

CSP certification is not mandatory to have a highly successful speaking career, but it can be extremely helpful to some along the way.

A Word from the President

Mark LeBlanc, president of NSA (2007–2008), started his company Small Business Success in 1992. He works with and speaks for groups of business owners and professionals who want to grow their businesses and sell more products and services. His website, www.smallbusinesssuccess.com, contains links to ordering his new book titled *Growing Your Business When YOU are the Business*, as well as a free e-letter called *Businesswise*.

Mark suggests two main strategies to grow your business or professional practice. First, stay focused on what you want: "Many in business today either focus on the wrong programs, products, and services, or are unclear on how to get more of what they want.

The more focused you are, the easier everything becomes, and you tend to get what you focus on."

Second, Mark is a firm believer in Dan Janal's service, PR Leads (www. PRLeads.com; see chapter 4 for more on this service), as am I. This service delivers publicity leads right to your inbox and also offers an article marketing service. "Publicity makes the world go round," says Mark. "If you want to get the word out about who you are and what you do, these unique and minimal investment offerings can increase the odds of a positive result and increase your visibility."

Mark offers one bonus piece of advice: "Focus on what you can do, not what you could do!"

A Quick Conversation with Mark

ANNE: Why should up-and-coming speakers consider joining the National Speakers Association?

MARK: This is the only association that exists to develop new speakers and help those speakers already in the profession speak more, have more impact from the platform, and put more money in their pocket. The sooner a speaker gets plugged into NSA, the sooner they realize that we help raise the standards of the profession with our emphasis on ethics, education, and our sense of community.

ANNE: How long did it take you to go from just having a passion for speaking to making a profitable living doing it?

MARK: Everyone takes a different path with their unique goals and aspirations. I was a part-time speaker for 10 years while I owned another business. I sold that business in 1992 and went full-time as a speaker, author, and business development consultant.

It's Not Your Grandfather's Toastmasters . . . .

Another pin on your map should be Toastmasters International. What images come to mind when you think of Toastmasters? Perhaps the old-boy network of stodgy old men smoking cigars and giving speeches in dark, wood-paneled meeting rooms? Today's Toastmasters is a 21st-century speaking organization and is certainly not your grandfather's Toastmasters club anymore!

Toastmasters is inexpensive, friendly, and supportive. Visit www.toastmasters.org and you'll find a hip and savvy website with pages of free tips, tools, and techniques that will help you as a speaker or trainer improve your overall skills, become more successful in your career, learn time-tested cutting-edge methods for presentations, increase your self-confidence at the podium, and reach your professional and personal goals.

Surveys continue to show that developing presentation skills, whether or not you speak for a living, is crucial to a person's success. Lots of people pay a good deal of money for speaking coaches and seminars to hone their presentation skills. Toastmasters offers a way to do this that is less expensive and held in high esteem in business circles worldwide.

Poking fun at itself on its website, www.toastmasters.org, Toastmasters has a section titled *What is Toastmasters? No, we don't make toasters*! Dues run an affordable $50 to $100, and most chapters meet once or twice a week. They publish the monthly magazine *Toastmaster*, and you don't even have to be a member to subscribe to it. Subscriptions in the United States run $20, and internationally, $30.

Scoop from a Toastmasters Insider

I spoke with Suzanne Frey, Toastmasters International publications manager, at their world headquarters in Rancho Santa Margarita, California.

Frey's advice to emerging speakers is to get involved with their local Toastmasters and experience firsthand all of the available resources and support. Frey also emphasizes that Toastmasters is not just for beginning speakers or business people wanting to sharpen their presentation skills. The organization counts many accomplished speakers among its membership and even offers a speaker bureau featuring top-drawer speakers to help local organizations fill their speaker needs, whether that be for a national meeting, keynote address, or storyteller for schoolchildren.

Frey says that Toastmasters groups are also formed in closed-club environments, like at The White House, in the United States Congress, and in *Fortune* 500 companies. "Wherever people want to participate in a supportive environment and help each other to be more effective in their jobs and more effective presenters in their community over all, Toastmasters can help," says Frey.

The Lawyer Who Would Be Coach . . . .

Debra Bruce is a successful lawyer coach. She practiced law in Houston, Texas, for 18 years, in firms big and small, then took her experience and started coaching other lawyers for a living.

On her powerful and hard-hitting website, www.lawyer-coach.com, Debra speaks directly to the lawyer in need. Navigating a career path in the law is hard enough, says Debra, and preserving a healthy life balance can seem impossible. But it's not. "I'm a lawyer and I know what you're going through and how to help."

Debra represents a growing number of professionals who have used their experience and talents to grow a different kind of practice for a living—professional speaking and coaching.

Debra's Lawyer Coach Tips

- Choose a niche where you already have industry or professional career experience.
- Ask yourself what challenges and concerns plagued you in that industry/profession, and be a continual learner and seeker of solutions.
- If you don't have industry or professional experience, educate yourself by reading a lot about the industry/profession and interviewing people about their experiences.
- If you do have experience in the industry/profession, keep reading and talking to people anyway to continue learning.
- Contribute your time to industry/professional associations and develop a reputation for reliability and trustworthiness.
- Get involved in other activities that include a lot of members of your target market.
- Write articles for the publications that your target audience reads, and interview target audience members in the process of writing.
- Don't be afraid to have a narrow niche. Clients seek expertise and experience on their exact issues.
- Find a community of others in your niche or similar niches (whether virtual or local) to share challenges and best practices with.
- Help other people succeed in whatever way you can. You'll build an army of supporters helping you to succeed.
- Build a good website with lots of relevant content for your target market.

Tips from an In-House Trainer . . . .

Anmarie Miller spent six years as an in-house trainer for one of the world's most popular, financially successful companies—Southwest Airlines. She is the consummate example of someone who transferred her presentation skills into becoming a facilitator for a training department in a large company—Southwest's University for People.

A Quick Conversation with Anmarie

ANNE: What advice would you give aspiring trainers about the many advantages to working with a training department within an organization, big or small?

ANMARIE: It's the opportunity of a lifetime to be in training—jump at it! Some of the best advice I ever got was to choose a work environment that meets your standards. Before making a decision to work for someone, make sure you look into the department and company you'll be working in. Is it a learning environment? Will you have ongoing opportunities for growth, like learning the development aspect of training?

ANNE: What did you learn from being a trainer that continues to serve you and benefit you to this day?

ANMARIE: The art of facilitation. I use this skill every day in all aspects of my life. Having been a facilitator helps me in making decisions, building relationships, communicating, and negotiating. I've also learned stronger listening skills, which is a key component to becoming an effective facilitator. Working as an in-house trainer is the best way to learn training and development from the ground up. Your opportunities will be endless, and what you learn in the process will change your life forever!

Advice from a Professional Saleswoman . . . .

In the field of professional sales, great presentations and speaking skills are a must for you to be successful. Natasha Beach is one such professional; she works for a worldwide performance improvement organization, managing and growing existing and new sales relationships, specifically in the federal government marketplace.

Natasha maintains a positive, highly energetic approach to her career in sales as a strategic account manager. "I work with a large military client, which requires that I kick off high-level sessions on the purpose, process, and payoff to working with my organization. Knowing that I make a difference every day in people's lives is what motivates me to keep going. Also being able to work in the

Natasha's Guide to Audience-Centered Presentations

1. Open with something relevant to the audience that makes them laugh. It energizes them right off the bat and makes them like you.
2. Make the speech about *them*, not about you or your company. You can certainly integrate part of that, but nobody likes a long commercial.
3. Keep it concise. Whether it's dinner or awards, people want to get to the good stuff, meaning the food or the awards, so their attention spans may not be that long.
4. Before speaking, try to mingle with the audience. Again, it's a way to connect with them that makes them more receptive to what you have to say, and also it helps you feel as though you have a friendly face or two in the crowd, which makes speaking in public much easier.
5. Relax and have fun!

field of human capital is personally inspiring to me. My goal is to make every place a great place to work," emphasizes Beach. (See sidebar for her guide to audience-centered presentations.)

So there we have it: you can start off in one career direction and use your knowledge and skills to become a successful speaker. And there are many helpful organizations out there to help point you toward the same compass point: speaking for a living.

MAKING IT HAPPEN

- Join a professional trade association to increase your contacts and exposure to other successful speakers.
- Listen to the advice of others who didn't start out as speakers yet have built success in their own speaking careers.

 **Chapter 12**

The Life of the Professional Speaker

The mind is a wonderful thing. It starts to work the minute you are born and never stops until you get up to speak in public.

—John Mason Brown, Literary Critic

At the start of this book, I told you that this business was often a roller coaster ride of ups and downs. I think it's important to remind you of that message. Although the road to becoming a professional speaker and trainer may not always be an easy one, I can promise you that it is an adventurous one filled with enormous gratification and personal reward. I have met the most amazing people on my speaking tours. And there simply is nothing more thrilling or exhilarating than standing before an audience and then connecting with that audience. How do you know you've made a connection? You feel it. So although it may not get easier,

215

I·can promise you that with practice and study you will continue to get better and better at this craft.

I have provided you with many valuable and real-world speaker resources. I hope that you will study them all and use them as tools to start building a profitable speaking career of your own. Plus, there are many great articles and more helpful information available at www.garrettspeakers.com. These helpful insider's guidelines and articles are include information on working within the meeting industry, the importance of customizing your presentation for all audiences, how to know who makes the best speaker for an event, and how bureaus find the right speaker for the right audience at the best price. Check out these tips and tools and follow the lead of industry pros if you want to join in their ranks.

Another resource is a series of products called *The Wealthy Speaker*, by Jane Atkinson. I like how Jane started chapter one of her book with the words *Reality Bites* and then launched into real-world scenarios you can expect to find in this business. *The Wealthy Speaker Workbook and Planning Guide* and *The Wealthy Speaker Audio Book* are also good selections for your speaking library.

Anne's Five Cardinal Rules for Delivering a Great Speech . . .

I have four cardinal rules I follow to ensure that my performance will be top notch. They are simple rules, but for me they set the necessary foundation upon which I can perform at my peak when conducting any event.

1. **Eat.** Food is fuel. If you don't eat, you'll be weak and you may even feel faint. Weak speakers don't go over well. Speakers who faint are not too popular, either. A dynamic and memorable presentation is going to require all the energy you can muster. A small meal a few hours before you go on is like putting fuel in your car.

2. **Sleep.** It's the original sustainable energy. When you sleep, you charge your speaker battery. You'll look good. You won't have bags or dark circles under your eyes. You'll think clearly and you'll maintain a high level of energy and momentum that will sustain you all day long.

3. **Breathe.** I'm not being sarcastic. You've got to breathe so that you feel it in your belly, not just your chest. I know speakers who get so wound up and nervous, they haven't drawn a deep breath in years! Do some deep breathing exercises to relax before your presentation. Breathe deeply through your nose and hold it in for five seconds, then exhale and blow it out of your mouth. Do this a few times and guess what happens? You'll actually deposit more oxygen to your brain and when you do this, you'll not only think more clearly, you'll be quicker, sharper, and better able to think on your feet.

4. **Get Turned Off!** Turn off your cell phone and the switch to your cordless lavaliere microphone or headset. Can you imagine giving a presentation and your cell phone starts ringing? And once you are hooked up with a cordless microphone, be sure the on/off switch is turned *off* until right before you walk on stage. When that switch is on, everything you say or do will be heard by others, including that last-minute visit to the restroom.

5. **Be 100% in the Moment.** Pray. Meditate. Be silent before you go on. Ask your higher power to help you to help others. This calibrates your intuition to connect with the audience.

Insider's Tip

To help ensure that my presentation will be everything the clients expect, I always supply them with a pre-event questionnaire (see Appendix B for a copy of this questionnaire or download a Word version from www.astd.org/speakforaliving that you tailor to your own needs). The questionnaire is several pages long and gives clients the opportunity to tell you exactly what their group wants, what is acceptable or unacceptable, or any sensitive subjects to stay clear of. It also provides you with important terminology you might need to know that relates to the group's industry. A pre-event questionnaire urges clients to consider ideas and focus on their specific objectives and desired outcomes, and then share those specifics with you. Once you have this information, you can customize your presentation to meet every goal your clients have set. This will result in your speech being a huge hit!

Room Set Up

Whoever books you to speak will ask you how you would like your room set up. If you are the keynote in a ballroom, obviously that is going to be set up for a large crowd. But for workshops, training, and executive meeting presentations, you may want tables in the shape of a horseshoe, round tables set for six, half-table set ups, patio arrangement, classroom style, or auditorium set up, and so on. There are many ways in which room settings can be arranged; think about which style would work for your particular presentation.

As you gain experience in this business, you'll discover that room set ups greatly affect the interaction that takes place—for instance, a classroom workshop, or a class that has a lot of ongoing exercises with people moving about, or a class in which you want to avoid distractions for more intense learning. With experience you'll get a good feel for what works and what doesn't regarding your particular style of delivery and facilitation.

Off-the-Cuff Speaking Opportunities: Just Say Yes! . . . . . .

You have to be spontaneous to survive in this business. If an out-of-the-blue opportunity presents itself for you to speak, just say yes. Relax. Delivering an off-the-cuff speech can be easier than you think.

Tips for Winging It

1. *Trust yourself.* You're the expert. You've been doing this a long time. You don't need notes to practice. You just need you, your mind, and your self-confidence to draw on the information you know so well. Trust your instincts and natural abilities for starters.

2. *Think 1-2-3.* Take one subject and then focus on three specific points that you want to make. For each point, write down three action steps for accomplishing the goal. Organize these three thoughts on the back of one of your business cards and work them in as you speak. Any presentation outline should fit on the back of a business card.

3. *Speak with personal conviction.* Believe in what you have to say. Drive home the points you want to make with compelling enthusiasm. Your audience will be riveted.

4. *Use a current event or a popular movie scene to make your point.* Start out with something everyone can relate to. Connect your subject with something well known and popular. Your audience will get excited if they can easily relate to something timely and topical. This also makes you memorable by association.

5. *Use emotion.* Relate a personal or emotional story to your subject or a key point you would like to make. Personal

stories are remembered long after statistics are forgotten. Did you know people retain information when they are moved to laugh or cry when given an example?

6. *Memorize a few unforgettable quotes.* Use quotes of famous people for instant credibility and implied endorsement of your topic. Audiences are impressed with speakers who can quickly connect the words of respected experts to their speeches.

7. *Speak intelligently.* You'll never be at a loss for words if you stay on top of the latest business and industry trends. Demonstrate your wealth of knowledge on current events.

8. *Engage your audience.* Don't just talk. Learn to facilitate responses from people. Ask them questions and then ad lib from their replies. This shows that you can think on your feet and make the experience interactive for audience members.

9. *Be honest.* Tell your audience you are winging it. Show your human side and you'll gain their undying support. Remember, audiences want you to be a hit! Be confident in the fact that you look and sound good. Don't doubt yourself.

10. *Pour your energy into it.* Speak up. Give it your best shot. Get passionate about the issues and tell it like it is. Enthusiasm makes you a more compelling and desirable speaker.

If you have the chance to wing a speech, you'll learn a powerful lesson—no one is ever going to know that you don't know everything they assume you do when you're doing an impromptu presentation. So just wing it and when needed, use these tips to handle this special communication challenge. The goal is to sound and look polished without warning. It's easier than you think.

This Book Was Written for You . . . .

I believe that if you truly want to make it in the business of speaking for a living and possess the talent required, then you can.

If you are passionate about professional speaking, then do it and don't let anyone talk you out of it. With passion for the business, you can inspire, lead, educate, and bring people to their feet to take some kind of action. And doesn't the world need more people like that—people who stand for something and take action?

As you grow your business, widen your experience, and gain more professional contacts and knowledge, you will prosper at levels you may never have thought possible—writing books, coaching, creating more products, designing and developing more seminars and workshops, and traveling the world. You will become your own mentor, so to speak.

Be Your Own Mentor and You Will Succeed Beyond Measure . .

I happen to believe that all books need companions, just like people, if they are to be more effective and influential. So I am going to recommend a companion book to this one, my book called *Be Your Own Mentor.*

This book you are reading now will give you the nuts-and-bolts reality of how to build a profitable and successful speaking career and business. On one hand, it's the professional go-to guide for making this career change happen. *Be Your Own Mentor*, on the other hand, is the go-to guide for establishing your personal endurance and fortitude for making it in this rough and tumble business. It will not only help you to set your personal course for success, but it will give you the tools you'll require to tap into your greatest potential as a platform performer, speaker, and trainer. It's a book that will further ignite your passion for the life-changing experience of building a profitable speaking career.

Being on the Rope . . . .

Years ago there was a famous daredevil circus act known as the Flying Wallendas. Karl Wallenda was one of its leaders and circus tightrope performers. One of his famous quotes is: "Being on the rope is everything. All else is waiting to perform."

I love this quote because it so accurately describes what it feels like to be a professional speaker. When you get out there on that tightrope—or stage or platform—being in front of the audience is what it's all about. Everything else leading up to that moment is simply about preparing and waiting to go on.

Welcome to the world of speaking for a living.

MAKING IT HAPPEN

- Know the cardinal rules—eat, sleep, breathe, unplug—for great speech delivery.
- Everybody benefits from putting all expectations on the table.
- Delivering an off-the-cuff speech can be easier than you think.

APPENDIX A

SPEAKER BUREAU
NETWORKING TOOLKIT

There are hundreds of speaker bureaus in the world. To give you a head start on what could be a daunting task, I have provided a Speaker Bureau Networking Toolkit online for you (www.astd .org/speakforaliving). The toolkit gives you helpful information that I have gleaned from my years of experience in the speaking field. This sampling of resources will start you on your way to establishing your own personal criteria for which bureaus you may want to represent you.

Remember, do not submit an e-blast to these organizations. Take the time to get to know them so that you can figure out the best fit between their clients and your talents.

- **Speaker Bureaus:** I have provided more than 150 top bureaus and their contact information, complete with address, telephone numbers, email addresses, websites, and brief description of each firm's niche in the market. You can directly hotlink to their websites using the downloadable PDF.

- **Trade Associations:** Learn more about the trade associations important to your speaking career; check out the thumbnail descriptions of these organizations along with all the information you will need to contact them.
- **Books and Publications:** Continue honing your skills and taking your speaking career to the next level with my recommendations for further study and reading.

APPENDIX B

SAMPLE OF PRE-EVENT QUESTIONNAIRE

ANNE BRUCE

SPEAKER • AUTHOR • CONSULTANT

Client Name: _____

Name of Your Group/Organization: _____

Website Address: _____

At your convenience, please complete the following Pre-event Questionnaire so that I may properly research and customize your program to meet your specific needs.

1. The title of your event or retreat:

_____

Is there a theme or focus? Please elaborate:

_____

_____

_____

_____

2. Date(s) to be held: _____

3. Location of event: _____

Address: _____

Phone: _____

Website: _____

4. Explain your agenda and breakout sessions, including times:

_____

_____

_____

5. What will take place before my presentation? _____

_____

_____

6. What will take place after my presentation?

_____

_____

_____

_____

7. What other training sessions will be taking place during your event? _____

_____

8. What are your three most important objectives for my presentation(s)?

1. _____
2. _____
3. _____

9. What would make my presentation more meaningful to your group?

_____

_____

_____

_____

10. Are there any sensitive issues or topics that should be avoided?

_____

_____

_____

11. What have you liked most about speakers you have had in the past?

_____

_____

_____

_____

12. What have you least enjoyed about speakers you have had in the past?

_____

_____

_____

13. What will be the attire for your organization's attendees at this event? _____

_____

_____

About the Audience

Your input here will help me to better understand the dynamics of your organization's specific culture and group make up. It does not in any way affect the content of the program. It simply helps me as the presenter to better serve your specific audience.

14. Estimated number of attendees: _____

15. Percentage of males: _____ Percentage of females: _____

16. Percentage of managers or supervisors: _____

17. Percentage of senior or executive level leaders: _____
Other: _____

18. Group age range: _____

19. Others who may attend the event? (clients, spouses, contractors, vendors, and so on.) _____

_____

20. What are the names and titles of your top leadership who will be attending the event? _____

_____

_____

21. Is there any industry jargon or terminology I should be familiar with or recognize? _____

_____

_____

About Your Organization or Group

22. Describe your organization's culture.

_____

_____

23. What are the greatest challenges your organization or group is currently facing? _____

_____

_____

_____

_____

24. Who are your primary competitors? _____

_____

_____

_____

25. What areas or regions does your organization or group serve?

_____

_____

_____

Name of person who has completed this questionnaire:

Name: _____Date: _____ Phone: _____

Please fax or email this information to:
Anne at 801-729-1144, or email to anne@annebruce.com.
Any questions, call Anne at 214-507-8242.

Thank you for your assistance. Your valuable input will
help to ensure the success and effectiveness of this presentation.

ABOUT THE AUTHOR

Anne Bruce makes her living speaking and training all over the world. Her workshops, titled *Speak for a Living!, The Good, the Bad, and the Ugly of Getting a Book Published,* and her popular *Author's Life Retreats and Seminars* are presented internationally and have helped hundreds of attendees launch successful speaking, training, and writing careers.

Anne is a bestselling author and inspirational speaker and trainer on the topics of human behavior, leadership, customer care, communications, employee motivation and retention, professional development, and personal growth. Her workshops based on her inspirational and personal growth books, like *Be Your Own Mentor* and *Discover True North: A 4-Week Approach to Ignite Your Passion and Activate Your Potential,* have been taught in seminars and at conferences from Las Vegas to Washington, D.C., Geneva to

London, Dubai to Delhi, and at business conferences and international meetings and management forums around the globe.

Anne is the author of the bestselling communications business book *Perfect Phrases for Documenting Employee Performance Problems* (McGraw-Hill), *How to Motivate Every Employee* (part of the McGraw-Hill Mighty Manager Series), *Motivating Employees* and its companion book *Building a High Morale Workplace* (McGraw-Hill), and leadership bestseller *Leaders— Start to Finish: A Road Map for Training and Developing Leaders at All Levels* (ASTD Press).

Anne has appeared on the *CBS Evening News with Dan Rather* and on the *Charlie Rose Show*. She's worked extensively in broadcast journalism and has been interviewed by distinguished print media, such as *Newsweek* magazine, *USA Today, The Times* (London), and *The Wall Street Journal*. She's been both a guest author and featured speaker for The White House, the CIA, the NRO, the Pentagon, JetBlue, Southwest Airlines, the Conference Board of Europe, GEICO, Coca Cola, Sprint, Blue Cross/Blue Shield, Ben & Jerry's, the Southern Company, and Continental Airlines. She's instructed programs at both Harvard and Stanford Law Schools and hosts her own radio talk show called *Anne Bruce Life Coach* in several major media markets domestically and internationally. Most recently, Anne can be heard as part of a success series conducted by well-known authors and aired in Cairo, Egypt. Anne also offers one-on-one speaker coaching to "kick start" a person on their way to building a profitable speaking career.

For more information on speaker-coaching sessions, workshops, and keynote presentations associated with this book and others by Anne, visit her website at www.annebruce.com for details on how you can bring this program, or one-on-one coaching into your organization. You also can email her at anne@ annebruce.com, or call 214-507-8242, for more information.

Anne and her husband, David, live in Charleston, South Carolina, and enjoy the beach life with their two 100-pound dogs Tex and Heidi. Anne continues to be recognized for her highly entertaining and award-winning platform speeches to multinational companies worldwide and is currently writing her first novel and screenplay.

INDEX